Author photo by Paul Neads

Gerry Potter is a poet, playwright, director, actor and both creator and destroyer of the infamous gingham diva Chloe Poems. A favourite son of Manchester and his hometown Liverpool, he trained at Everyman Youth Theatre and National Museums Liverpool lists him amongst the city's leading LGBTQ+ icons. His published works are included in both the poetry and philosophy collections at Harvard University and the portrait documentary *My Name is Gerry Potter* premiered at Homotopia in 2015. He has a reputation for putting his Scouse voice on the line and is strong on poetry and strong on the causes of poetryism.

Planet Young
Gerry Potter

Flapjack Press
flapjackpress.co.uk

Exploring the synergy between performance and the page

Published in 2009 by Flapjack Press
Salford, Gtr Manchester
⊕ flapjackpress.co.uk f Flapjack Press
🐦 FlapjackPress ▶ Flapjack Press

Reprinted 2010, 2013, 2021

ISBN 978-0-9555092-3-0

Cover design by Brink & Gerry Potter
Cover photos courtesy of the author

Printed by Imprint Digital
Exeter, Devon
⊕ digital.imprint.co.uk

A UNESCO City
of Literature

Dedicated to Paul Butler [1952-2006].
A brother. A hero. A comedian.
With love from me and all our family.

Thank yous.
Thank you.

Contents

Foreword

Anyone who's seen him knows Gerry is an excellent performer. He always was. From playing every possible cameo role from old sea dog to seagull in an Everyman Youth Theatre show when he was fifteen, to the misanthropic old crank in Jeff Young's *The Burner* (can I hear "typecast again?"), he has been compelling and inventive and vital. Watching him perform his poetry as Chloe Poems was more than a 'reading', it breathed a whole dimension into his words. That meant that when he gave me *Universal Rentboy*, his first book of poetry in 2000, I expected to read it like a theatre programme, keep it as a souvenir, a reminder of the 'actual' work. But the poetry stood up on its own. Lines shone out of it and found a new resonance. Rhythm remained. The choice of words was pinpointingly accurate. It was funny and heartfelt and angry and political. I realised just how good the actual work really was.

I first met Gerry in 1979 at the Everyman Youth Theatre. He was my friend's uncle (I mention that because it lends me youth). He bounded into the already eccentric room wearing Mork braces and a Doctor Who scarf and a pair of red Kickers and how could I fail to love him? I don't think he really noticed me, but his best friend Brian fell in love with my Alice in Wonderland dress and a perfect love triangle was born. When I saw Brian and Gerry perform 'Lullaby of Broadway' in full drag on the stage of the Everyman Theatre a couple of weeks later, I knew no other men in frocks would do for me.

After running away to Glastonbury for a year (where else?), they walked back into the Youth Theatre like celebrities, greeted as returning heroes who'd earned another stripe on their braces (or notch on their cowboy boots in Brian's case, but that's another story for another gay). We were in the best possible place, the Everyman Youth Theatre, № 9, hippy old Hope Street, top of Food For All, Hardman Street, Liverpool, the 1970s, Planet Young. The place where we could be exactly who we wanted to be. And at the Youth Theatre, all of us Young Romantics touched each other metaphorically and literally, held each other up to the sky, taught each other to fly, fed each other's souls and egos. The freedom and beauty and possibility of that timeplace is in this book, crystallised in ink, transforming blank pages into the essence of youth and the potency that is the potential of the very soil of Planet Young.

Since then, Gerry has been to Harvard, cruised Canal Street, proclaimed himself not camp, fought with taxi drivers, become Chloe Poems, worn a jazz cardi, lost a best friend, fucked many men, lost a Mum, written 'The Queen Sucks Nazi Cock', lost a(nother) brother, killed Chloe off and become Himself – with a capital H because he was only ever himself, now it's just that he's even more so and has poetry to prove it. He has also invented characters like the absolutely loveable Tiffany Bling, the awe-inspiring Audrey Pringle and the difficult to translate Folly Butler. Except they're not invented; from Gerry's heart they bleed and become as real and as vivid and as vital as Treeza Woosey and the Sons of May Butler and the Million Mothers of Vauxhall Road.

So what's his secret? Well, the reason the books work is that Gerry is not really a performance poet. Like all great writers, Gerry is a performer whose voice is always present in his work, it performs itself off the page. Gerry's poetry is the distillation of his life, animated by his intellect and his remarkable understanding of words and their play. Reading the work is like hearing him perform it; it always finds its author's rhythm, but reading it to ourselves allows even more room for all the possibilities of his language to articulate themselves because they reverberate off our own experiences. It also gives us a chance to rewind, to go over those parts of the performance we missed, because we were too busy laughing at the cheeky rhyme or the audacious pun of the previous line. And as we do so we become more intimate with him and his world, because there is always more than the surface joke and there is never an easy rhyme for its own sake. There is always a deeper meaning.

You may never have been drunk at the Youth Theatre disco, or been an effeminate in Scottie, or unable to sleep, or dreaded Thursdays or have encouraged an Innocent to eat your mum, but somehow you will have been there and you will know how it feels, because that's what good poetry, what great art, does: it puts into words those niggly thoughts at the periphery of your vision and the edges of your mind and makes sense of it, it nails it down. It allows us to imagine and re-imagine and feel and remember and live other lives, some of them our own. All this by daubing brushstrokes in an empty space. And that's what Gerry does so well. His brushwork can appear haphazard on the surface, but the more you look, the deeper you go, and inevitably you find the old master; another love song to humanity.

This book is a real gift; it is the gift of ideas, the gift of wit and the gift of yourself. Most precious of all, it is the gift of youth. Welcome back to Planet Young.

Maria Barrett

Introduction

OK, here we go.

Above all, I wanna chat. I want this to be a kind of conversation. Not just this, the so-called 'Introduction', but the whole goddamn book. I love talking, always have, but also love response and it's hard to get a response from you when you're not here. So, this is me chatting to you, albeit an invisible you, and this is how I talk, kinda bitty and all over the place. Hope I'm talking to lots of people – that will mean this book has sold a fair bit and I'll end up getting a shiny bob or two. I'm not a money-motivated animal but am old enough to realise good times don't buy themselves. Those halcyon, neon-lit nightclubbing days, when little more than a wiggle of one's once-pert disco tush and a cheeky beckoning smile could keep me out for a whole weekend, are long dusted.

It's exciting having new books fall into the world, always feels like partying, like raving. Raving's kind of what I've been doing with these poems and myself for some years now. They've been dancing with their hands in the air like they just don't care for too long. It's high time they landed and that's how all this creatively feels, they and I have landed. It's time we cared.

For a blurringly long and meaningful time, I was up in the air as gay, socialist, transvestite poet Chloe Poems. Some of you might have heard of her; an alter ego of an altered boy and my drag extension from Liverpool to Oz. Chloe was The Gingham Diva, radical agenda bender and Voice of Treason. A once daring, dancing with danger doyen of undergrounding intent and counter-cultural shenanigans... the darling head-butt of mayhem. The kid girly voice I was abused for and accused of having, all growed up and iconoclastically defiant. It's fair to say for two high-energied decades I lived not only a double but also a chequered life.

Chloe's gone now, never to return, her pathways open to anyone wishing to tread them. Also, I'm getting older and Chloe Poems was a proactive, nu-waving, gingham punk, an eternal teenager if you will, wildly of the time and should never age. There's something about having been someone that will never age I find personally powerful (perhaps my new drag persona should be Crystal Methuselah). I'm as an anarchically proactive a thinker, but experientially aware I'm a lot less youthful. So, in these greying days I do what I do in a gentler manner. It was the right time to say goodbye... more goodbyes later.

A lot of what's presented here is in a peculiarly poetic form and that can sometimes leave some people bemused. Some people have more than delighted telling me I'm one of the more idiosyncratic poets, a critique I can agree, own and contentedly work with. Chloe and I owe far more to Mummers and The Beats than we ever could Shelley or Keats. Yes, I'm a tricksy occasional rhymer who believes performance poetry has as much right to be historically documented as any other incarnation of the art form. So, approach the work like lyrical storytelling, staggered poetic prose, theatrically nuanced monologue... improvisationally informed theatre-verse.

I was brought up in a much-talking house, within a much-talking family, in a much-talking community. Even as a child I knew intricately personal things about people they never knew I knew. Jangle drizzling, downpouring in a mizzle of spurious conjecture, dazzling rumour, piquant rancour and generous hype. In Liverpool we call conversation/gossiping "jangle". In Liverpool we think jangling sometimes haphazardly and accidentally profound. I sincerely hope this book jangles.

Liverpool's Scotland Road, or Scottie Road, or just Scottie as it's sometimes affectionately known, was and still is a stuff 'n' stumbling area of caustic repute. When I was '60s/'70s growing there, it was designated one of the toughest areas in Europe. It's why I'm now immovably atheist, because no loving omnipotent God would ever put an obviously effeminate homosexual kid in a Catholic secondary modern in 1970s Liverpool. Only an impotent, sociopathic, homophobic sadist could be responsible for something as excruciatingly brutal as that.

For some reason (and that reason must be the Mersey and her docklands), Scottie Road has an almost folk-sung, folkloring, mythical quality/tradition. Stories/songs are still affectionately weekend romanced and trilled by well-soused Liverpudlians who (no matter how blind drunk they expertly are) always find a way to get home. There's many a ribald tale and mourning shanty proving its historically embedded, booze-enthused, working-class credentials. If you put your ear to a nearby conch, you may just hear one now.

Names are important. This book has lots of names, some getting explained, others not. We forget names, sometimes we wish we could forget more, but, good or bad, some names stay with us forever. I don't read many books; in fact, I've not voluntarily read a book for some time. Reading's difficult for me, but I find listening easy. Listening is a lot like reading. If we thought of the world as a library and we, the people, were its books, then I'd be considered incredibly well-read. So that would make people books and books have titles, meaning our names would be the title of our books. So, by me merely mentioning a name, I hope you're getting the idea there's a lot more biographically present than just a fondly remembered moniker or indeed, Monica.

This is my first book as this name, Gerry Potter, and these words are in my voice. It feels good to say that and I can't quite tell you why. I don't mean that in a secret-keeping kind of way... after all, we're jangling. Mmmm, the irksome enigmatic thrall of the narcissistically imponderable, I guess it keeps us on our toes. And as a first book, I suppose it has to tell my story. Safe to say, I've lots of stories, far more than this and no less important, but these are the ones queuing up and camping outside the January sale of my mind (a lot of my stories camp) – first come, first served. Being from Liverpool, my gob is part estuary, big and wide, so I'm sure there'll be more to spill one day.

This first tome explores what I call the domestic/fantastic. Domestic/fantastic is something I often discuss with my dear friend and godforsaken Mancunian Gary McMahon. In some poems we're wearing domiciled real clothes of a life well-worn. In others, we outrageously drag-up and trip into disco lights fantastic.

I believe in lies. I believe in truth. In some way we're all a perplexing Janus façade and cunning 'where's the lady' coin trick, we are all drag. These two companionable contradictions have merged somewhat successfully since a good woman met a bad snake and ate an apple, or so I was always humbly led to Eve.

Although there are many somethings, I genuinely believe everything belongs to nobody and in the end nothing is gloriously/ingloriously all ours. I've put these musings onto paper and, if you're reading this, I sincerely hope what's written, these sea-salting bursts of language, become in some small way, yours.

It's a world, things happen. This is how I've based my whole ethos. I've just started writing and this has happened and I'm not going to change a word. Well one day, maybe a little.

So read this book like we're having an early evening drink, just taken a trip and you're listening to me waffle on. Or if preferred, read it like you've taken an E and you are endlessly telling me the ins 'n' outs of your incredibly eventful life story. Whatever your choice invisible you, I promise I'll listen; you're a book, remember. Jesus Christ, read like you freakin' well want, I'm only a performance poet damn you! A verse vaudevillian, a be-stormed trouper on his drugged/drunken way back to a beleaguered windswept cellar club Oz. So, who am I to dictate?

I do hope you find in it some of what I've put here. Because I'm pretty sure I must have put it there for something.

Gerry Potter

Planet Young

My Scouse Voice

Chloe Poems was a bit on the posh side and spoke differently to me, so when deciding to drop her I could no longer write with or in her voice. After years of performing poetry, this is the first poem I had to write for and as me.

My Scouse voice takes off like a Jumbo Jet
set for Heaven, carrying its roar on winged prayer.
Jesus is in there, so are Mary and Joseph,
a religious motif kicking like a mule.
Schooled by gravitas, failed by school.
Gravels like a death rattle arrogantly assuming resurrection
and sometimes can't be arsed meeting makers;
it's protection from the worst laid plans of movers and shakers.

Sounds honest, even when lying.
"Honest!"
No denying the conviction it can carry if it needs to escape.
It'll convince you statues can fly while drinking your drink,
making you think you're listening to your best mate.
Runs through sewers,
floats on updrafts of gossip and jangle.
It's passionate about Mrs Mullaney not getting her paper that day!

I love the way it bounces off walls 'n' ricochets
like a hail of neon bullets in a hall of mirrors.
It brothers sisters,
a family of flat vowelers partying in sing-song intonation,
dances in hotpants, has nothing to prove,
one thousand intonations under a groove
with kick-assonance attitude.
A pop-cultured reference, rock 'n' roll heart 'n' soul 'n' rude.

It can hack like a rack of seagull beaks peckin' y'ead,
Bangin'!
Clangin' like the hangover from Hell.

I've seen men-mountain crumble
as the missus humbles them to the consistency of quivering jelly.
Witnessed its underbelly,
raw dark aggression and obsessive assertion it's better than you!
Rock hard 'n' dockyard,
happily bite off more than it can chew.

Has a soulmate in decadence, instinctive eloquence
forged from the world and its words,
such serious resonance then Nelly the Elephants
absurds.
Rallies, rails, succeeds, fails
in integrity of conviction, free 'n' jailed,
cast off and set sailed in the adventure of any direction.
So fast it blurs, Rabelaisian slurs, inebriate nights on the town,
cares, caresses, confides, confesses,
will try not to bring you down.
Fragile as a broken smile, comedy 'n' bravery.
An oral tradition of wit and guile, dipped in the horror of slavery.
In a milkman's whistle, worker's song,
hard-arsed gristle, right as wrong,
the throaty cough of legendary birdsong.
A Liver Bird on sixty a day,
it's international, it's straight, it's bi, it's gay,
a multitude of everything, even Walter Mitty,
a choral sound of the profound and gritty.
Unconventionally pretty, inspiration for many a ditty,
a choir for the city.

I've heard it gibbering the unbearable bubbling of grief,
a melody wavering heavily round my youth.
Sounds like a dark room without the telly on,
babble of ham-fisted sandwiches
pickle sweet smellin' in 'n' out of whiskey and incense.
Definite as death, dreamy as nonsense,
I've heard its absolute truth.

In pre-teen sounds of a thousand nephews
clogging up Christmas Days, laughter lighter than air,
startin' to develop that inimitable drawl
and in drunken redundant caterwauling unities
of football harmonised pub-crawls.
I've rode its register from laughter to tears.
It's my Scouse voice and still working-class after all these years.

It's the charm of a traveller,
sailor's hornpipe jigging 'n' boisterous.
An' the only time it pisses me off
is when people who aren't from Liverpool try 'n' do
their Scouse voices.

Battered Blue

For put down and upon Doctor Who fans everywhere and everywhen. In the wilds of Scottie Road, five television programmes stopped me from going mad and, indeed, made me gay. They were The Tomorrow People, The Naked Civil Servant, I Claudius, Rock Follies and of course Doctor Who. The title of this piece is lifted from Terrance Dicks's (author of many Doctor Who novelisations) description of the TARDIS being a battered blue police box.

This is the story of Battered Blue, the boy who wanted to disappear,
get the time and space outta here.
Unable to fit his surroundings,
bored of the poundings 'n' name calling
and crawling a snail pace to that appalling waste of space
called school.
He thinks everybody in there's somebody's fool,
how he hates his lumpen quarry,
man-fisted specimens of macho sorry whose only worry
seem to be girls and training shoes.
Got those, he's had enough of those, far too much of those
beleaguered, brittle, battered blues.

Strain visible on his young old face,
trapped in this place of fraught teachers and wrought iron gates,
caught in streetlights of bland landscapes
and the wheezing groaning of football.
It's all he can do to keep it together,
knows it won't last forever,
even at the end of his tether
Battered Blue never says never.

Because he's seen the future and the future's free,
an endless stream of thought and possibility,
of warp ellipses, temporal anomalies,
radiophonic colours of eternity.

And a hero who won't let him down,
who's been around for over nine hundred years,

whose word he's always heeded,
who fades and appears just when he's needed,
who he can trust in and confide.
Who knows,
Battered Blue is so much bigger on the inside.

He's seen galaxies form from twinkles in eyes,
sleeps under a blanket of alien skies,
supernovas keep him company as he dreams 'n' flies
the intricate weave of space-time.
He can fit universes on the head of a pin,
get caught in the middle and begin to find a way to fit into his grin
and become the man in the moon.
His constant companion infinity with forever in the vicinity,
he's someone,
he isn't,
he is,
isn't he?
He's the why in the wherefore of now.

Reads of himself in tomorrow's news,
in his eyes imprints of a trillion views.
She's the spark of a match, he's Dorothy's shoes
and just wants to save the world.

Treeza [1961-2005]

Chester-born Terry (Treeza) Woosey was one of Liverpool's most raucous characters and Madonna's biggest fan. He/she could make a group of people fall off their chairs with just one witty comment. I know, because I was there and still cherish the bruises.

If Madonna could really perform miracles
rather than just make money, then I wish she'd bring you back.
I miss you.
Miss the hacking attack of that fiendish laugh,
infected and infectious.
Miss our blonde/brunette banter,
the Cagney 'n' Lacey of closing time.

Miss getting pissed in The Curzon,
that hole in the ground bar where pornography goes unnoticed,
more like wallpaper than passion.
Where you met Mr Fluff and got married.

Miss the drag/drug haze and spirits of Christmas past,
the way you so completely got Gill,
Robbie and Susan,
"Socialism Tommy",
Linda McCartney's sausages, remember?
Remember you were the most beautiful woman in the world.
Words bold as vodka 'n' lipstick,
lipstick, lipstick, lipstick,
lipstick, lipstick, lipstick,
lipstick...
far too much lipstick.
Red raw acoustic,
unplugged.
A caustic bitch no man could resist,
you thought.

Miss you howling at the moon in sixties donut earrings,
laughter orbiting the stars,
scarring our crepe paper validities of outer space,
off my face.
Shooting stars illuminate the black hole,
distant and remaining.

Miss you singing "Hello Young Lovers",
arms outstretched and window-framed.
You were impossible gold girlfriend,
my heart is a dog-eared coffee-stained.

I miss those great chunks of my past,
detaching
like I'm on a rock watching the landmass passing by,
carelessly and precariously
attaching themselves to somebody else's life.
Remember.

Tiffany Bling

Portrait of a scally girl.

Tiffany Bling wishes she could sing songs sung by singers
she can't pronounce the names of.
"Mutty Banana" springs to mind, who's really Mutya Buena,
ex-Sugababe gone solo.
Never wishes she could go that little bit further
and write her own songs.
Doesn't like listening, never mind writing,
fighting's more her thing for her life or anything.
Tiffany Bling.

Never used the word universe,
speaks in riddles, free verse, nonsense 'n' cliché,
never rehearsed,
unconcerned and carpet-burned she lights another ciggie.
Likes hip hop, the chip shop
and to kick off when no one's listening.
Screwed up Tiffany Bling.

In full swing Tiffany Bling sounds like a catfight.
Saturday night lasts till Wednesday morning.
No flirting or fawning,
just the noise of crushing glass,
boys,
screaming and falling apart.
Doesn't know much about art but knows she doesn't like it.
Doesn't know much about art but if it fucked her off she'd fight it!
Not one for critiquing.

Moira Brogan called her a tart,
she broke her nose really hard.
A lesson taught thought Tiffany, off to court went Tiffany.
She fought the law and the law won,
accusing Tiffany Bling of almost nearly killing.

Didn't turn her back on O-Levels,
just couldn't face them.
Never diagnosed for the depression fogging school grey and red.
Its floor a parquet swamp she would wade 'n' rage through,
the lava mud in her head she gave way and sunk into.
Wants to get married, an engagement ring.
Sparkling Tiffany Bling.
Can't eat apples, misses her mum, calls asylum seekers scum.
Teeth hurt, need filling.

Wants to marry Brad Pitt, doesn't really know who he is.
Thinks she's never properly kissed
and laughs at people's misfortunes
in the same way she laughs at cartoons.
Wouldn't know what to do with an epiphany,
knows nothing about the economy,
a little about astrology and wishing.

Wants to buy a baby called Portia
and Brad would have to learn to drive.
Misses the baby that haunts her and to live on floor five,
John F. Kennedy Heights.
Must buy a new pair of tights,
she's got more ladders than a window cleaner.
Wonders if the boys have seen her.
Embarrassing Tiffany Bling.

Her mate Janet, who lives on another planet,
wants to go out, said so on the phone.
She's all green skin, feathers, antennae, tentacles,
rah-rahs and boob-tubes.
Tiffany buys a litre bottle of vodka, a rock, and new shoes.
Loves partying!
Tries to find the bus, it's missing.
Calls Janet who lives on another planet
"That funny Miss Ting inni'."

Tiffany Bling's off her head and kicking cars,
not allowed in bars, shouting, swearing at shooting stars
who keep whispering her name.
Screams "You're just there to do me 'ead in!".
Shiny studded nasty men nailed to the black of thought.
Thinks she can count at least ten laughing at her lack of acumen
and inability to walk.
Throws a punch and then knocks out two ambulance men
talking that spongy talk,
blood's spilling, she's misting.
Doesn't know what she's created or she's being sedated,
just the colour sound of panic, dulling.

Has never known a sweet thing or the songs she can't sing,
indeed what's happening.

Poor old Tiffany Bling.

The Qualities Of Mersey

Have we ever truly looked out, completely beyond
what we are, could or wanted to be?
Stood, harbour-cold facing everything's of other?
I wonder, can we,
am we,
I wonder, are we.

I'm big on blasts of salt, how sea tells you you're there.
How she thinks your thoughts everywhere,
filters them through breezes.

You get this feeling space knows
what we are, could or ever wanted to be.
Sometimes I'm space shaped,
an invisible outline of mere-maddening imagery.

October damp and blagging I get it all.
Sea tells me, I get it all,
a tricksy, flighty witch, whispering secrets oversold.
She's big on floods of economy.

I like she's cruel, a sinker; I like she knows she can.
Makes me a bad man, home dark and housed.

Perhaps they're waves of tears,
those auld folk-sung poetics,
songs of others tuned into air.

Why it's sound, the how 'n' what we hear
and where it's meaning.

I Never Went To Eric's [1976-1980]

Eric's was a club, slap-bang in Liverpool city centre's Mathew Street. It was always and still is legendary; a counter-cultural, underground Mecca with an improvisational ethos not only for new music but new people. The wildly creative punk/reggae Bohemia it generated made Liverpool the most exciting place to be a teenager – and although I never actually went to Eric's, it felt like I might because so many people I knew did.

The air was honey soot, apple tart,
lit by the crimson starlet of Margi Clarke.
It played daft tricks, blew salt licks,
lapping like a seadog panting.
Somethings were inventing a brand new city.
Rain sweet thought puddled the pavement crazy,
men in suits hadn't pin-striped its last breath yet.

I was naïve sixteen, wet behind the ideas
and its Tolkien structure inspired, ripened.
It was enticing, a wizard's den inviting,
magicking me in seventy-nine,
undeniably mine and impossible.
No one told me I wasn't immortal,
no one told me I wasn't important
and still had hold of all I had to lose.
I cruised.
Punk had bollocked, frolicked 'n' fuelled a new wave,
semi-permanent 'n' Twinkie.
I was breathing with it, singing succinctly its song.
Liverpool was a soft as silky iron lung about to exhale
a blizzard of golden kisses, a ballad of so far yet so near misses,
the sea-sure sound of washed-up wishes.

I never went to Eric's but Dalek I Love You. John Cooper-Clarke and Siouxsie Sioux. Betty Vampire knew Marx and Lenin. The Grapes, Yates's and the White Star. Bands sharing beats and hot chocolate in the Kardomah. Stories unread, stories of the blues. Lennon's big bang creating news. New Romantics putting their slap on, sexed-up scallies grabbin' grannies down The Grafton. Part fire, part tricks, part heaven, Pink Military on the march, dancin' in dungeons, larks in the park, Boxhead's flat-top a hotwired ginger spark. Whether The Pistols did or didn't, it's immaterial, Holly Johnson was Judy Garland and mercurial. People were cookin' da books 'n' lickin' da licks, people were dissin' Thatcherists. Echo and the Bunnymen at the Everyman Bistro, stunning, Toxteth alive 'n' burning, running the media riot, we were the anti-quiet encouraging the shushed-up to wake up and try it. On a clear day the Welsh mountains, me mate Ian in The Pale Fountains. Jayne County apocalyptic blonde, dangerous and fraught. Remembering second-hand Lou in dusky Déjà Vu and the beautiful Colin in Food For All, our food for thought, who poured far more tea than we ever bought. The Everyman Youth Theatre spawning a million eternities, a million courses, Roger Hill reigning over a chariot of shining, brilliant seahorses. John Knowles, Brian, Dave, Helen Teabag, Kim, Lyn, Angie Sammons, Brenski, Graham, Vic, Jane Buchanan, Richard Johnson, Jan, Jan, Jan and Shirl. The Human League without the girls. "I wanna be tall tall tall as big as a wall." With all the improbable twists 'n' turns. The fire of Probe and the Pat Phoenix of Pete Burns.

The air was honey soot,
salt as oyster, sweet as jelly babies,
alive with the definites and the maybes.
Culture home grown not imposed,
unfinished unwritten not done dusted and recomposed.
A forgotten renaissance,
so it goes.
Now I know why teardrops explode.

All wrapped up in change.
All wrapped up insane.

Just Off Chaos Grove
An ode to Hope Street.

Vibin' that jive just off Chaos Grove,
a heartland of lit,
where the hot 'n' found diggin' into,
lost it by breakin' out 'n' through and bringin' it.

We hear it colour sounding by numbers,
dancin' on clouds and knotting rainbows,
you never forget the sighs of those uplifts.

Chaos Grove grew stuff,
showed not told, glowed not scold.
Sat cross-legged on the corner of Love Precipice,
opposite our sweetshop's red neon soul.

Young thrice at Chaos Grove, mother of all mothers.
Gave birth to Methuselah the Teenagers,
life to the tribe.

Planet Young

This is based on the photobooth picture my good friend Lyn sent me from years ago – the photo on the cover. Lyn also came up with the title (ta, Lyn, you've started such a ball rolling). This is dedicated to the life changing/enhancing Everyman Youth Theatre and photobooths, places of so many adventures and perfect environs for teenageing.

Make no mistake, nostalgia's a stake through the heart;
photobooth 1980 March.
Three lives, different hair, posing for the camera
for a future of posing.
Eyes wide, relationships forged,
molten metal, steaming water, bubbling under
the plump fluffed skin of cheekbones.
Wild-eyed boho and hormones, the juice of life is experience
but there's a twist and it goes like this:
Liverpool still smells of the sixties and its achievements.
Pissed on a vodka and Halloween memory,
pulled down trousers at the Anglican Cathedral,
that sexy bisexual milkman Kim introduced me to.
So handsome and cerebral, he fancied me,
wished I'd kissed him.

Prepare.
Preen.
Pose.
Giggle.

We feign stunned, look cute, know each other completely.
Lifeforms inhabiting planet photobooth,
visitors landing for a short stay on Planet Young.

It's all very Gary Numan and Janis Joplin,
hippy 'n' Nu Wave.
Snoggin' posh people at posh house parties
in posh parts of suburban Scouse.

No idea of romancin',
just dancin' 'n' neckin' 'n' kissin' 'n' gropin'.

Loving being aliens.
I'm Tom Baker, all teeth 'n' curls,
Lyn sultries Cleopatra,
Brian does camp eyes with far too much behind them.
Probably raining, pavements steaming, we were reigning,
best teenagers in the world.

Had sex but haven't.
Surprised how many girls fancy me.
Brian howls a cackle, reduces us to tears; different tears then.
I'm hovering in an orbit of a sometime when
somethings always happened.
About to plummet to Planet Earth,
Tippy Tumbles time travel all clicks, clunks and whirrs.
Space Invaders sum up the time.

Four poses.
Three people.
Three people for posing.
People who'll disappear.

Flash!
Flash!
Flash!
Flash!

Grey curtains forcefield us from the world,
Lime Street space station, actually a train station.
Love trains, like spaceships always going somewhere.
Can smell rain and the docks and leftover after shavings
of other people's chat up lines.

Why wasn't Dave there?
We loved Dave, his mum was so kind and grieving.

She was tea, biscuits, sandwiches and welcoming,
she made her home ours.
I fancied one of his brothers.
His Grandma looked like Mrs Christmas, smelt of flowers.

I hear us laugh clear as belles, vibrant, meant.
Laughter shapes suns on Planet Young.
We do drama, circle games and improvise.
Played out my life story last week.
We can touch each other with our eyes closed and it's not sex,
closer than anyone else.
Tied up in trust, trussed up in tights and the promise of theatre.
The smell and wet of photos drying, bit like stink bombs,
wave them like a damp flag.

Meeting Angie soon, queen of giggles,
High Priestess of The Beatles.
Gonna liberate her from school, kidnap her to Southport,
our showbiz island.
The pier turns Brian into Barbra Streisand.
We sing, dance, laugh and take on the world
with our take on the world without the weight of the world.
Shabby immortals,
mummified youth,
timeless,
calcified in a strip of black and white.

    Drip

                drip

      drop

                 drop.

They're tears falling onto the page.
You have to type out teardrops on computer paper.

Carl O'Prey loves Rock Follies.
Brian's favourite, Rula Lenska.
I was Julie Covington cos I had the badge.
Last week The Rocky Horror Picture Show changed our lives.
Last week was over thirty years ago.

Nostalgia's hard.

Honestly, sometimes, don't like being adult, too brutal,
not human enough, not Gary Numan enough.
Can I stay alien, vivacious, unassuming?
Orbiting Planet Young forever today.

Queen Rita

There was The Everyman Youth Theatre and there was Bold Street's Café Tabac.
Places where the soul couldn't be freer or soar higher... and there was, of course,
Rita.

Stood her ground at and with you, sound la.
Scouse Shiva givin' it her own private Shangri-La.
Shooting with the hip, shouting with a quip,
always ship-shaped and pristine fashioned,
she outrun a tidy fleet

From autumnal stumbling in to greet,
Rita'd meet you with an eye or smile,
on wry days, both,
double-barrelled was her middle game.
Honesty her oath.
Didn't need prisoners to take,
all of us willing hostages, spilling sinners,
but woe betide you getting too familiar.

An angled postured glare from hotter sides of the sun,
shone till giggling beginners froze.
She could make those freshers take big steps,
she could make them take tiny steps,
her groove, her choice, her shows.
Oh that voice had reach,
preach and the generous subtleties of teach.

Lady with an attitude, lady with face,
lady with hat 'n' shoes,
her banger special gave great taste.

A titanium oven-gloved velvet pinched hint
of diamante sass.
Shimmying a simmering/sizzling butch-zhuzh diva
and glammed up jazz.

Even covered in flour, she'd Dietrich and Holliday.
Movie stars do fry in Liverpool.
She'd gorge the goulash 'n' juggle the five-spice.
Brian and I would giggle as we always giggled…
"'Ave ye noticed babe,
she never has the same hair twice."

Twelve of us, one table, most of us gay,
a rapidly diminishing flapjack, a multi-refilled pot of Earl Grey
and one helluva just-cast spell, you'd hear our roars in Hell.

If she wanted us shoo'd we were booted,
if she wanted us rooted we were suited.
I like my wisdom bold knowing
with wickeding hints of precise slice.

Heart-shaped ice goes *plink plink*,
sinking in with pink gin'd punk-denim mohawkery
and inexpensive vintage corduroy.
There were days I couldn't believe I was living this life,
could feel this much joy.

Y'should have seen it in there,
psychobillies giving aquiline curved acetylene hair,
All of everything and its outsider'd cousins,
as eye of storms go, it was fuckin' buzzin'!
A hangover cure for the shipwrecked,
an anarcho-sitcom ghost-written by Brecht.

When remembering,
it explodes with partying supernova'd force.
When Josie Jones gave sly eye, tables erupted.
Being busted and reconstructed by destiny
is the sauce.

And of course her hats, every leader an obligatory crown,
she had that linear milliner'd style bang down.

Café Tabac written atomic neon red and silhouetted
in front of her signature, Queen Rita, of the glitter sweet.

Razor-sharp, tailored displayed matriarch of Bold Street.

Gone Fission

For Ken Campbell [1941-2008].

In 1979 I joined The Everyman Youth Theatre and it changed my life. In 1980, Ken Campbell became artistic director and he changed my life. He brought with him Neil Oram's The Warp and what was already unbelievably amazing suddenly became anarchically fantastical. An incendiary influence.

In shine of a supernova made blinding by Ra,
Little Baby Ken shot cockney-eyed from the cunt of a star.
He blistered 'n' blustered formulae and theory,
he blasted 'n' bolted and very nearly changed the world.
I think he slept in a kaleidoscope and chipped in on the wheel.

Clearly knew his voice, dearly loved to use it.
Really loved the mind, knew how to Blues it.

There are parades where your feet strolled,
ideas burning 'n' sparking.
Teenagers who are now old
are still larking around singing your praises.

Oh, how mighty those little acorns grew.

You made us giants and children.
Giants and children, Ken
and giants and children knew.
They know!
They sit atop and stare down,
playing.

A city sits up, hears you shriek ideas.
A city steps up to the peak of its powers.
A city opens its mouth and swallows you whole.
A city knowing base metal is a city knowing gold.

Colour!
He re-booted colour.

The Everyman became everyone and everyone everything,
everybody a merry dance and every brain cell jigging.

A totally eventful horizoning.

The jazz-bang of your theatre rewrites time
and nuclear energy is human.
It was spectacular
burning in the White Star of your love.

Human!
He re-booted human.

Neil Cunningham [1943-1987]

The Everyman Youth Theatre, 1981, and we're doing a Johnny Speight play, If There Weren't Any Blacks You'd Have to Invent Them. I was to portray an aged, blind racist. Neil Cunningham, an actor in Ken Campbell's Everyman repertory company, very kindly offered to show me how to do an ageing make-up. It was and still is one of the finest hours of my life. His late-night cabaret show, Metaphysics and Strip, was one of the reasons I found performance poetry.

An Everyman dressing room and I'm in a chair,
he's a confidently theatrical homosexual,
it's 1981, you could be then.
I'm to look old, older than nineteen
and it's more exciting than Christmas.

Neil has swan hands, elegant yet bouffant,
an arch arc illustrates his fingers,
half bird, half cathedral,
a forty-a-day honey-opera's choraling in his voice.

Smell of Leichner clings,
like lichen made from Marlowe, pitch perfect projection,
teeth 'n' tits.

In complete awe and have been for two years,
theatre does that to a young mind and heart.
This is an actor of such standing, stature and film
and I'm just this Scottie Road wannabe upstart.

He's warm witty,
outré carved from charm 'n' meaning,
anecdotes eloquently pour through decorative flirting.
Tells me it's impossible for skin this young to look old,
so we shall have to mask bold, shade and define.

Words new, sentences leaden with stage history.
Thought spirals travelling through mystery.

Tell him he'd make a great Doctor Who.
Aside-mouthed, he snarls *Don't be piffling darling,*
that reductive crap's for amateurs.

The hour embers, ambers,
crackles a Dickens'-Victorian,
alive's like we're being ghost-written.
I'm being taught without rage,
being shown without telling.
For the first time I feel grown up.

Half-dances around,
a witty ballet of graceful harmony.
His eyes are woven wisdom, wrinkle-embedded and shining.
He's showing off, airy, fairy, subtle as a breeze.

In our reflection, he's behind me,
bulbs around mirror, hands on hips he says
See handsome, what did I tell you?
It's impossible to make you look old.
Let's let age do that shall we.

One Moment Please

Out of time the moment steps,
a breathless Ruby Keeler about to become a star.
You hear them in dreams, weep for them pissed,
but some moments shimmy a cha-cha,
demanding attention and belief in an afterlife.
Moments tonguing the cheek,
cheeky moments, rah-rah, almost Dada,
camp as drag queens' Christmases.

A bold moment uses the last of its three well-heeled wishes.
Wishes it was with you in your life,
butting-in like a too tall gatecrasher with boundary issues.
Inaudible loud like memories of shouting parents
or those bands you hated on Top of the Pops.

This moment de-legs you,
wobbles you like a Weeble not falling fall down,
this moment begs you listen.

This moment won't tell all, whispers in double-dutch.
Whispers secrets of whispering,
holds romance of memory close to its chest.

Doesn't tell you the Lottery numbers
or even its name,
knows you're addicted to mystery, anarchy and empathy.
This moment knows you well.

Brian [1964-1995]

Brian King was my best friend. We did everything together and were kindred inseparable. This is about the grief I still feel and, in many ways, how proud I am of it and of Brian. It also charts the loss of my last semblance of religious or spiritual faith.

I'd like to think of it as a collage of kaleidoscopes,
unfolding, uncertain, flowery, yet stoically there.
Breath forged from marble,
a kiss on the cheek from the Invisible Man,
a spirograph starcharting destinations and afterlife.
I'd like to think it's not and never been goodbye,
a heartbroke song from an aching mum or sister,
like it's not and never been about alone.

I'd like to think of it as a lock unpicked by a hairgrip
not quite opening but you can peek inside.
I'd like to think of it as the godly man in frothy beard
and robes made of stories and wine,
or as ambrosia music,
melodies forging a pathway through the custard smoke
of Vaseline-smeared longing,
winding down, spiralling out.

Like it shouldn't matter you're alone,
because somewhere there's a seaside photo
of communion blessed nirvana 'n' eating doughnuts
and in the chaos of a distant fairground I can make out your tune,
Chaka Kahn singing 'Ain't Nobody'.
I'd like to think of it as a continuation of a very good time.
I'd like to think of it as a lie, like it's never left me without love
and needing the personality of matter.

I think matter really matters.

Like it's never been about being alone!

Hey kids,
it's a trumpet of hugs and kisses blown gracefully
from our avant guardian angels who've left their wings
and credibility indoors.
I'd like to accuse the ferryman of overcharging,
I'd like to think Death Nell and Grim Rita
are drag queens overacting.
It's jokes without laughter, gossip without words
and Brandy 'n' Babycham doesn't drink itself.

I'd like to think all that prayer is stored in a library somewhere,
volumes of thought and intention just waiting to be read,
borrowed or turned into something blue.

I'd like to think you're haunting the places we danced.

In my dreams you wake up with me.
Do the dead dream of the empty living and does that mean
I wake up with you?
I'd like to think somehow somewhere there's a place for us.
I'd like to think you could think outside that box
and the knocking I hear occasionally in my tower block
are Morse coded hellos, not the wind.

I'd like to think it's a race you win rather than lose
and there's a solid ground that doesn't seem
so faithless a starting block.
A solid ground of ghosts made real
and death doesn't have to happen.

I'd like to think angels paint stars
and rocket ships superimpose on your face,
but I never wanted infinity, I think.

Just to grow old together.

Brian And Gerry
When memories collide.

In 'n' out holiday car crashes, diamonds in seas of coal,
north stars with necessity inside them, showbiz shenanigans glitter.
Where wicked witches moon-bathe, hobgoblins kiss 'n' tell,
magicians tell of legends and hillocks full of God.
Clouds miming double acts, fairy lights twinkling rage.
In hysterical small talk of secrets our Aggy paints us live art white.

Dave, Ian, Jackie, Louise, Wolverhampton, Shirley and Jan.
Thundercloud boyfriends feign understanding.
Mickey and Maria roar giggles,
squabbling because squabbling's a talent.
Unities of unique.
One word best friend making empty rooms sing.
Be billionaires if we could sell smiles.
Ever seen earthquakes row?

Mary Carney's laughs lit neon.
Two cathedrals, one street, makes sense,
something total can be subtle.
Within electric beige experiences
Christine 'n' Mandy government topple.

His mum a feast of pies and pasties,
brilliance like Mary Carney's laugh,
like Mickey and Maria's roar,
jam in marshmallow moons.

Ian danced the eccentric, Jocelyn stitches time,
Lindsay holds and Robbie's warm as embers.
Acute triangles, whiskey shots, improvised everything,

kingfisher flash.

Laurel and Hardy. Sugar and Spice.
Sun and Moon. Brian and Gerry.

Drag. Poetry. Outrage. Laugh.
Plenty Sparkle. Plenty Handbag.
Brenda Handbag. Brenda Backcomb.

Adorable. Understanding. Cryptic. Grave.

Paid. Afraid.
Laid.
Laid.

May cried with knowledge.
Jeff looked the saddest.
Lynn Pop wailed like a mother,
laid out he looked like Fozzie Bear.

Clip –
Flip –
Slip –
Tip –

    and Hardy.
    and Spice.
    and Moon.
    and Gerry.

Odette Du Poetress, Chloe Poems.
Sex and Violence-Theatre Like Life.

Tracy sung her blues and See-Ann dressed as an angel.

Volcano [1921-1997]

My mother, May Butler, was many things, but above all she was experienced. She never left Liverpool, seldom left her area. For thirty years she never left the house. My mother saw four of her eight children die. She saw two adult children die within a very short space of time. She brought up most of those children on her own. Ours was a hugely loving and often difficult relationship. This poem starts at age five and somehow ends at sixteen. As a young child, I'd sit behind her watching old films. Writing this poem surreally felt like writing half-remembered, strobing, monochromatic old movies. The Chinese Empress (whoever she was) is one of my earliest telly memories and all I nearly remember is I somehow wanted to be her.

1.

Sometimes dream Chinese, dreaming of being English,
daydreaming of being royalty.
A most important dream allowing me to surf planes of hypocrisy,
journeying flights of infantasy till arms tire, running out of steam.
Love steam, don't dream of steam enough.
Its hissing impatience allows a gloat of unknowing,
empowering a conceit;
I often say to strangers, is buried but never died, never going.

Content with catatonic pretence, knowing I'm not the only one.
Nonsense. Belong to communities of pretenders
who know pretending not to know is art.
Intense splashes of non-colour, kaleidoscopic,
tipping a-tumbling, blurring, juggling.
Becoming kinds of truth, violence.

Nonsense, intense violence.

"We are all made of lies."

My mother, more of a man than my father,
who spoke in tongues of molten lava told me this.
I believed her, this four-foot ten behemoth.

This motormouth of one tooth also said
"Gerard, lies are made of truth."
How she'd yin/yang her words,
this black/white Chinese Scouse empress
who could fight rabid boar, feed five thousand,
comfort the depressed, roar like a lion imitating a mouse;
proud of a house furnished by debt,
who taught children to say no, middle name,
Volcano.

2.

Often awake, dream for dreaming's sake,
a superhero in a cape coping with natural disaster easily.
X-ray eyes, arms elastic, super strength,
tripping off lights infantastic.
Escaping evil with blurs of super speed.
it's a need, a secret,
hides my identity, stops me shying away,
flying away, throwing keys away
and retreating far too far into my fortress of solitude
hidden in Volcano.

With broken pencils I draw me
perfect,
not like a girl but all muscles and bravery,
draw myself strong enough to save me,
a manly master of altitude impervious to pain.
Unafraid of silence, can hear everything,
worms singing nursery rhymes, tocks between tricks of time,
ready to face the nonsense, intense violence.

A butterfly wings out an S.O.S.
A caterpillar combs its hair in readiness.

Pretend not to know life is fierce and I am weak,
sometimes pretend I'm unable to speak.

Trying to be accepted, trying to like football
but Emma Peel is so much better.

It's trying, trying, trying.

Trying poetry, yawning, doesn't talk like pictures.

3.

Why must we testify love, can't we just say we're lonely?
Why make it benign when it's furious?
I've a great idea: it's Wednesday, let's pretend to forget it rages.

I see saggy thoughtless lumps of damp defeated squibs.
A brown paper bag envelops an airtight tin.

I was told love worked for my grandparents.
Children believe the dustbowl history of lies
where lie ad lib libraries of ad hoc ancestors
always getting it padlock right.

She lights the blue touch paper and I reluctantly stand back.
Sparks fly directionless,
sharp, bright, adolescent, arrogant.
Flash white black reminding me of my parent
and the untouchable she couldn't teach,
corners she couldn't reach.

Vesuvius crackles blue red green,
November sixty-seven, Heaven!
Five years of age and never more elated,
I start to understand fantasy.

I hold her hand and with total honesty
testify my love for fireworks.

4.

Grief.
Different for me.
Although her seventh son, I was eight.
It was wild, exciting, not unlike a party,
not unlike a firework display,
not unlike surreal times fish.

Volcano had lost her fourth child,
second in six weeks.
Thomas, twenty-one, twenty-two the next day.

Tears are ash engulfing memories,
scorching images of her dead onto cheap net curtains,
pink.

Eight and the world's cracking up.
A gash of pouring blood truth,
thicker than tears,
blood.

Lots of men are red-eyed.
Those who are not are teaching me how to fight, how to box.
Although I'll never use this knowledge do so enjoy the lessons.
Men are kind and I have never felt so Catholic.

My handsome cousin lifts me trophy high.
Peter.
I'm giggling, excited.
Looking down I see my brother in his box.
Thomas.
He's frozen smiling, don't like it.
Peter calls him handsome, remembers our Jimmy,
starts crying.

There's tea, alcohol and hyperactive women doing too much,
never seeming enough.

Not unlike a party,
not unlike a firework display, not unlike
flashing teddy bear rail track dead.

Volcano's collapsed, no longer a Chinese empress,
a goodbye-ing pale,
Little Miss Hollow Mountain.
Stalactites form from her tears,
evolving into the bars I will one day look out of
longingly needing to play.
She needs me more than ever, more than forever it seems.
Eight and I face an eternity of grief,
an eternity of...

Transported to a desert and sat dressing
Action Man in Barbie's clothing.
Sun's behind, slow setting,
extending my silhouette like a heel of a stiletto
across the sand.
It's the long hand of a clock, strong sound of a tock.
It says "Chloe, grief is the shadow of love."
Don't know what it means, must've have misheard it.
Why did it say Chloe? My name's Gerard, eight.
Seventh.

5.

Escaped school, singing a pop song,
'Do Wa Diddy' springs to mind.
Tenement steps are Hollywood stairs,
glittered not littered, leading to a top floor Emerald City.

Oscar nominated again, spot-lit illuminated.
I've a picture, a daffodil and an Easter chick,
perhaps it's the start of the holidays.
Memory like schoolboy pockets,
full of holes, string and small change.

Still singing, must be the holidays,
wouldn't be trilling so triumphantly
if school were trouncing tomorrow.

The horror of P.E. scarier than Christopher Lee.

I reach the top, front door ajar, unusual.
Dance into the living room,
Anne Miller out-stepping Judy Garland,
tapping my blues away and wishing my pumps had heels.

Volcano's asleep.
Usual.
I squeal,
"Mam."
She stays asleep,
odd.
"Mam!"
I giggle.

Giggle fades, joy's bleached,
streaks, stinging my tongue.
forget every word of my acceptance speech.

Dormant.

Touch her shoulder,
head drops.
Feel fear supernova and find voice.
"No, no, mam, no, please!"
Grab her with more hands than I own.
"Please."
Falls forward.
"Please."
Falls forward. Doesn't stop falling forward.
Falls forward.
"Please."

Don't know what to do. Need to get help.
Falls forward. Can't leave her alone. Need to get help.
Too many hands.
Falls forward. Can't leave her alone. Need to get help.
Yelling screaming.
Falls forward. Can't leave her alone. Need to get help.
Is this death.
Falls forward. Can't leave her alone. Need to get help.
Easter Parade. Peyton Place. Emmerdale Farm.
Falls forward. Can't leave her alone. Need to get help.
Call the police. Don't have a phone. Sooty 'n' Sweep.
Fred Dinage.
Falls forward. Can't leave her alone. Need to get help.
Need the priest. Farmhouse Kitchen. The Galloping Gourmet.
Falls forward.
Falls forward.
Paint Along With Nancy. Susan Stranks.
Falls forward.
Falls forward.
Falls forward.
Afternoon Plus. Kreskin.
Falls forward.
Falls forward.
The Cedar Tree. The Sullivans.
Falls forward.
Freezeframe.
Close up.

Glitter bleeds from ruby slippers.
Never felt so me before.

Her face flabby, a damp paper bag.
I watch exhausted.
Numb.
Still.

Still?
"Mum?"
A twitch, the sliver of a sneer, a snigger cracks the cold.
An erupting mocking roar, what's happening?
Can't know what's happening
because nothing like this has ever happened before.

Resurrection.
Must be Easter.

This is the day God went mad.

Can't know what's happening, my brain's too small.
She's laughing, holding ribs laughing.
Caterwauling as I'm smalling,
calling me stupid for crying, telling me I'm like a girl.
She's lying.
See her mouth, her one tooth clear,
a tombstone in a poppy field and want to punch it out.
She's calling me a stupid little queer.
No map to reference,
no counsellor to call, no wailing wall to smash a hole through.
Small.

Nonsense, intense violence.

Insurrection. Change.
Heart snows over, my tears and I ice age.
It takes seconds to evolve, a hardened criminal.
Diamond.
Planning my first big job.
She's just murdered a child, I might murder her.
Remove silk stockings, American tan glitter-flecked,
slowly slip them over my head.

Drop my Easter picture, my daffodil, my chick.

Wasn't wanted, so I squash singing into gelignite
and plan to blow up fantasy.

Living, breathing, laughing, she goes to make my tea.

6.

Wow!
I'm a mother child, like a girl,
telling stories to make a mother woman sleep.
It's cosy dark, blanket musk beautiful,
blank canvas of night-time sweetness.
The screeching stops, Disney'd birdsong greets us,
violence, nonsense, even the sirens nightingale.
Pain melodies away, making way
for fairies, goblins and Old Willow Pantomime,
witches, poo monsters and Chinese Scouse empresses.
Tell a different story every night, a tell-tale temptress,
sing a different song.
Time to take your agoraphobia flying 'n' rocket tears to the moon,
who needs pocket calculators, Etch-A-Sketch or Buckaroo?
This is the finest gift, the best.
Here in bedtime it's love and rest.

I'm beginning to perform,
an author without writing a word,
just voice.
Our family find it disturbing, call it absurd,
their choice.

An eleven-year-old parent starting at eight,
sending his mother to sleep.
We secrets keep.
I know my job, lessons school couldn't teach.
School would've laughed, "You're like a girl!"
School cruel, mocking my voice,
a high-pitched camp ant chirruping, sibilant, lisping.

Arrogant mimicking making me embarrassed to speak.

In this peculiar real I hold the reins.
I'm Magic Man in these tiny hours,
an invisible girl with special powers,
a superhero fighting real life crime.
Your child,
your mother,
once upon a time.

7.

Sometimes dream and it all comes stumbling down.
The way it was and how it could have been,
conundrums forged in hell,
freefalling downward and *splat!*
Dream sometimes and it all makes perfect sense.
There could be no *never was*, there could be no *never could be*,
a tale spiralling sideways,
an unmagical spell, an unmitigated history
and that quite categorically is that.
Sad as happy, useless as important
and all the revisionism in the world is foggy.

Double act,
more Judy and Billie than Morecambe and Wise,
we holidayed in fantasy when reality hit.
Abstract,
two different faces on a double-headed coin,
so clumsily ragged, so snug a fit.

I mat, you cat, fat smothering, auburn grey,
unable to wander, determined to sit.
Moth, moon, vampire and bat.
Two orbitals stuttering, whisperers muttering,
nurturing fluttering, dimly vivid as lit.

And all the revisionism in the world is...

Volcanoes, mountains, lava gorged, rumbling,
tornadoes, mother child, Kansas bound, hope forged,
jumble sale'd, grumbling.

We were all we ever could be,
all we ever were.
Mother, child and all the revisionism in the world
is herstory.

The Sons Of May Butler

My original name isn't Gerry Potter, it's Gerard Butler This poem is once again about my mother who, through tragic accidents, saw four of her children die. Two young children and two adults. This poem isn't about grief, it's about the way my family got through its grief. Somehow, we were still able to party, so this is a tribute to them all. My family were bang into westerns and this is based on John Wayne's matriarchal classic The Sons of Katie Elder.

Kinda hard to say it's sweeping majestic
but honestly sometimes that's how it feels.
Epic,
tiny,
a black hole in a snowstorm and when you shake it…
oh my God!
So much of it sixties monochrome,
so much of it seventies Technicolor and so much of it sleeps.
It's hard to get into its white noise obesity and reason out.
They were accidents waiting to happen weren't they
and accidents are part of life aren't they
and life is just an accident waiting to happen isn't it.

The Sons of May Butler,
Liverpool silhouettes,
shadows in the sunset of a scorched hard-bitten Scottie Road.
Such a magnificent seven on silver wing horseback,
irreverent red and blue hats like Scouse cowboys should be.

I try to make sense of it by being alone,
me and my imagination walking Liverpool,
lip-syncing the diary of my life.
Sometimes my mouth moves too much
and I'm sure people think me mad.
But occasionally get a nod from people I assume recognise
I'm a son of May Butler,
undocumented history with my band of brothers,
a Samurai story made North by North-western.

It's then I know I'm someone in these streets.
It's not just romantic,
a figure in a concrete Bayeux Tapestry,
part of a family cradled fondly in the empathy of bricks.

It can make me feel special, I mean really special,
other even, arrogant.
Sometimes it's like I know too much
but I don't tell anybody that.
It comforts and my skin tingles pinpricks of satisfaction
and such intense pride from just being a son of May Butler.
Make a brilliant film wouldn't it,
The Greatest Story Never Told,
historic like the Kennedys, hysterical as a Carry On.
Bags I be Charles Hawrtry but only in a biblically epic sense
("Ooh Matron"), and life must carry on, mustn't it.

Sometimes tell the story and I know people don't believe me.
It's like waiting for tumbleweed to take a bow.

The Sons of May Butler are charging through the city,
bareback muscle on stallions, quicksilver lightning the night,
want to set fire to things, they want girls, one of them wants a boy,
bite tops off beer bottles, eat the glass, drink hellfire,
spittoon diamonds and dance.
After all, oblivion's only a burning stagecoach away
and dancin' and singin' must be done.
"Makes you feel alive as a bar brawl, Gerard!"

I know it's fuzzy logic, a tied-up Gordian Myth,
Inn of the Sixth Happiness meets Cathy Come Home.
It's not totally thought through,
but we're still talked about in Scottie Road.
They say, "How did poor May Butler get through that?
Warra brave woman."

I remember Annie King, who also lost kids,
telling me she was remarkable,
and it does sometimes feel remarkable,
legendary,
big legendary like John Wayne.
Don't know who'd play me, but think me Ma would be played
by Ingrid Bergman or Jennifer Jones.

The Sons of May Butler
nooned high on the horizon, framed by desert dust.
riding the range,
weather-beaten, parched.
Skinned ruddy brown,
eyed steely blue,
keen as a cheroot,
determined and denim'd as bounty hunters
avenging a killing, writing a wrong, collecting their dole.
The drumming of hooves a Gregorian chant
and noise of a white hot city turns industry into an orchestra.
Music swells,
all smile at once and dazzle the coyotes.

They know what they gorra do!

Spurs spark kickin' into skin, silver wings spread
and song of feathers unfold,
descant and rise.
Well-heeled horses leave the ground and clouds of dust behind,
it trails for a little while
lending more magic than can ever be paid back.
Seven figures reach for the sky
rising above the fever pitch football pitch and buffalo.
They're the Sons of May Butler ripping through clouds,
tear-arseing the fabric of time.

It's oldest first, that's just the way it is,
Jimmy, John, Vincent, Thomas, Chris, Paul and Gerard.

I'm proud to tag behind.
The Sons of May Butler give the sky an alphabet,
whooping and hollering,
telling dirty jokes, bending their shapes,
turning horses into letters.
They circle the sun, move inside it,
not too close, just enough, they're not daft,
they're Butlers not the Icaruses.

They synchronise,
shifting,
forming words,
sun-blurred,
almost florid like a hard knock Busby Berkley.

And below from the plains of Scottie Road,
haloed yellow,
if you look up
You can make out the letters

M A Y B U T L E R

It's sweeping, majestic!
The sun of May Butler shining down,
just a little reminder lest Scottie Road forgets
the greatest story never told.

Drunks And The Ghosts

There's a full moon somewhere with my name on it,
like I Love Lucy, only butch.
Shining in puddles, bewitching like an ecstasy tablet,
a scene from Hobson's Choice,
a befuddled metaphor hollering nonsense,
a ventriloquist doll finding its voice and man I can sing.
Matt Monroe meets Oasis,
trippy shades of a thousand wonder wails.
All dummies can sing after their seventh Guinness,
born free, dance, twisting with a thousand imponderables
and an infinite capacity to rejoice.
And I almost always find it here amongst the neon and cobbles
and it almost always feels like yesterday.

And I've searched the library of my history,
that well-thumbed maze of truth and lies,
I asked the actors and dancers to mime it for me,
I've sought the stupid, stalked the wise,
I asked the socialists who turned their back on me
to soldier through shoulder to shoulder,
but money took them over too, what possessed them, I wonder.
And it seems wandering's all I've done,
I've walked the length and breadth of this land,
danced when I should've sat down,
encountered danger, animated the bland.
Slurred a million poems I can't remember
in ears too full of disco to hear,
something about transcending gender,
something about pride and queer.
And I asked the gays to build it for me,
of course I'll help lay foundations, but God's honest truth
it's just a fairy story,
so I'm left with these lamentations.

It's like pick 'n' mix with no choices in a sweetshop
made from science fiction and an alien's selling community
like a priest sells crucifixion and I want it,
I need unity, like capitalism needs addiction.
And I'll keep searching, go where no man has gone before,
lurching into dangers I sometimes can't control.
And I'll keep digging,
indefatigably digging,
even if it's an undiggable hole.
And I'll be brave enough to be frightened,
hear you call it denial and I'll make the rough enlightened,
diamonds for a while.
I'll point to the moon so they can see past the fight
and tell them to remember.
Nostalgia's gonna start tonight.
Nostalgia's gonna start toooo...

Good times and wisdom mixin'.
At least until the hangover kicks in.

And I almost always find my way
using these almost seen signposts
and they almost always seem to point to the drunks and the ghosts.

My Factory

Scottie Road was once surrounded by massive industry and the choke of workers. I was raised as its fodder. With the possible collapse of global capitalism once again in the air, I thought I'd re-employ this little moment.

My factory said
"Leave your wife, leave your family,"
so I left my wife and family.
My factory told me this was right,
my factory lied.

My factory told me to pull my socks up,
zip up my boots, ride my bike.
My factory fell flat,
tyred.
My factory died.

My factory found the key to my heart and mass produced its beat.
My factory rains. My factory cries. My factory leaks.

It speaks to other factories, tells them I am lazy,
tells them I've had syphilis.
It's not bothered if this will make a difference,
just plods and chugs, just Rods and Chucks.
Clogging the atmosphere with smogs and fucks
of what might have been and maybe.

Broke!
Unholy smokes of dirty jokes.
My factory doesn't know punchlines.
Throws punches, tugs hearts and pulls only string.
My factory lies between here and everything,
it's motivated by nothing,
says it's motivated by green.
It's motivated by the banal of the obscene.

I saw it in a party hat, couldn't dance for toffee.
I saw it in a suit, looked gnarled and baggy.
I saw it in trainers, mutton dressed as lamb.
I saw it in a mirror, preening 'n' pining.
I saw it in the gym, wheezing 'n' whining.
It was in *The Sun* with its tits out for the lads,
for the lads and the lads' dads.
It was in *The Sun* with its tits out for itself.

Chug-plod-chug-plod.
I feel sorry for my factory, pity.
Gives up on the ghosts it designs,
on the blokes, on the jokes, bleeds them dry,
between you, me and between the lines.
I wish it would give up.
Chug plod.
Shut itself down, get on its bike, unzip its boots,
give back to its roots, kill the suits.
Chug.
Blow itself to smithereens, fall to the ground, one out all out.
Plod.
My factory tick tick tick tick.
Chug.
My factory tock tock tock tock.
Plod chug.
Clocking in. Clocking on. Clocking off.
Clocking in. Clocking on. Clocking off.
Clocking in. Clocking on. Clocking off.
Plod. Alarm. Plod. Alarm. Plod. Alarm.

Strike! Bombsite.
Chug plod...

Fidgetin'

Dedicated to insomniacs who, like myself, seem to spend most of their time in bed fighting off the hideous strobe-like dementia of half-sleep.

Debbie McGee, Judy, iffy, like tummy ache.
Like a beleaguered breadwinner,
like a beleaguered breadwinner who's tired,
like ill, hobo like, cosmic,
like a cosmic walk, a comic walk, space walk.
Moon boots with stilettos.
Stilettos, y'hear me, stilettos!
Moon boots stuck in the cracks of doom.
Crack of Doom boots.
Dank, like damp, like dark,
like an alleyway run by rats and policemen,
by rats, policemen and local councils...
eatnibblenibblegnaw eatnibblenibblegnaw
eatnibblenibblegnaw eatnibblenibblegnaw.
Like porn, weird porn with brothers, with mothers,
not just our own mothers, like succubus, like cumming.
Like cum face. Auntie has a penis.
Like rain wet bread losing integrity, limp, jumpy, like startled,
like bright eyes, like headlights, lost in a forest, lost in a dream,
lost in a disco.
Doughy, like rain-wet bread.
Guilt like a kiln, baking, hot, like running, like sweating.
Chased, like startled, in forest, in dream, in bed, in Birmingham.
Sweating like Birmingham.
Wringing, changes, like corners in corridors,
like space hops, like sweetshops and sweatshops,
like last times and past times, like time jumps.
Debbie McGee.
Screaming, screaming and screaming.
Dreaming, sideways in time,
like Judy, like the Victorians, like garlands of flowers.
Who will buy?

Jumpy like Judy, crowned like Judy,
like thorns,
jumping like Jack.
Flash!
Like garlands,
like gardens of rabbits, like, bunny-cake,
like headlights, like running to the light.
Splat!
Like flesh, like car crash, like mum, like Judy.
Beans like pizza face.
Hit like hit
hit
hit
eatnibblenibblegnaw eatnibblenibblegnaw
Debbie McGee.
Garland.
Waking with hard-on, wanking like shaking,
no meaning, like dreaming, like living,
like dodging the beleaguered breadwinner.
Like running from school bus to school bus,
like hit
eatnibblenibblegnaw eatnibblenibblegnaw
eatnibblenibblegnaw eatnibblenibblegnaw,
earth quaking like sleeping.
Sleeping, like living, like waking, like sleeping, like waking,
like making a cup of tea.
Ow!
Like hot.

Winged

For Paulo.

There's this other me and he's handsome, strong, winged,
an ivory smiling, beguiling hunter-gatherer,
never lost for words or style.
Got this way of winking.
Cheeky.
Melts hearts and for a while he'll make you think he's yours.

His bravado opens doors and comforts strangers.
Doesn't make mistakes
and got this way of talking you can't not listen to,
magical, like he's telling stories.
He's reading a telephone book and it's like he's reading stories.

Invented Braille, unveiled the sun.
Believes we're all God and death's an eternal nap.
Lies on the ground so he can hear the Earth breathe.
Lies on the ground, soothes him to sleep.
Sees his reflection in clouds,
dreams perfection and thinks nightmares get a bad press.

Knows tomorrow like the back of his hand,
sees futures in everything.
Wrote the perfect pop song once on the back of a Penny Black,
stuck it on an empty envelope, posted it to The Beatles.
The song was about distress and people.
Found a rhyme for orange then just as quickly forgot.
Juggles melancholy and joy like a pro.
This other me's got the lot.

Abseils thinking,
sticks his fingers in the spaces of a snowflake without melting.
Once shone a torch,
discovered the moonbeam and turned a continent silver.

Can stop war with a wave of one finger
and baked the first apple pie.
Taught Father Christmas all he knew and baked the first apple pie.

This other me will always be there for you.
Won't make you cry or leave you to die,
it's impossible for him to disappoint.
Got this way of knowing almost everything I'm told.
Can juxtapose nothing with something
and come up with a Morse code dot dot dashing the stars.
Some say he's responsible for ABBA's 'S.O.S.'.

His career plan consists of being, there and yes.
Some think he's somewhere between madness and God,
or a pillow between a rock and a hard place.

Think I met him once in the corner of my eye
and we spoke just out of earshot.
We nearly had a cup of tea and he almost soothed my grief.
I think I met him once and we talked Freud and bubblegum,
looked through a photoless wedding album
and called the bride and groom ghosts.
It was in a café, Kim by the Sea.
We nearly sat at a table in the corner of my eye.
He almost had apple, I ate humble pie.

This other me lives in a community
with a whole load of other thems.
Gems of people who can levitate tables and wait on,
stay silent for years then craft a whisper from a roar.
Somehow more than human.
Changed the world.
It's written somewhere they reinvented science fiction
with nothing more than a piece of slate and a laser beam.
Dream in black and white then delight in colouring them in.
Bend light into ideas and for breakfast gorge on thought.
They're a one meal a day kinda people and gorge on thought.

Keeps a diary, it's in seconds,
each second has twenty appointments and never misses one.
Like I said,
doesn't do disappointments and he's never missed one.

This other me teaches statues to fly and negotiate rainbows
so they can see a multicoloured Earth.
Fleshes them out apparently as they glide effortlessly
with open heart and mind.
You can see them perched on churches, confident and grinning.

He's the spirit of a whim
whose billowing smoke spins tales in tailspin.
Beginning of a sentence at the end of time,
an occasional rhyme tossed 'n' turned in word salad.

Sings the ballad of the lonely,
whispers sweet somethings through rain
and lullabys rebel songs to sleep.

Folly Butler

Folly Butler talks in daffodil,
"Scremt thruppp sghart spreeek spreeek ofda,
ogla meek ogla meek oorimpta."
Which means,
"Hello petal, how goes your day? Here's to the sun on your path."
Walks in a song, has a giggle in her voice,
a city centre Alma Cogan once saving a baby from scalding.

Keeps company of secrets, tells stories tall as trees,
everybody's friend in waiting,
only says us, never says me and catches tears falling.
Hears tears calling.

Folly Butler butterfly kisses airheads.
Tells them,
"Birrakempt birrakempt tilsa tilsa dilly, mirriump skreep
skreepa lil mirriump, pileeli miskilleri miskilleri."
Which means, "Babe, it's all gonna be OK,
same thing happened to us only the other day."
Helps ice cream keep its cool,
makes the River Mersey dance The Twist.

Escorts shadows from cradle to the rave,
sending them up up up,
up and around the bend.

Blue Eye

A reluctant tribute to the cloying claw of unrequited love.

Hey Blue Eye promise you'll protect me from the storm.
Turn back the tide, hold up the sky.
Make the sun shine hope and roses,
shield my eyes and scent me crimson.
Blue Eye be Viking, flex muscle, make me a country,
cross ocean then conquer.
I've got this notion one day you'll make a cave of your body
and deep inside I'll whisper instructions of love,
whispers I daren't hear for fear of hearing,
little whispers of a hermit.
Blue Eye do me a favour, notice.

Hey Blue Eye listen to this.
I pretend to be a girl and we get married.
Not a real girl, I'm your blonde dream.
I have this notion of chickens, gingham curtains and everything.
It's really real, even the picket fence sings.
It sings, "Blue Eye ploughs the field and deserves apple pie,
Blue Eye tills the soil and holds up the sky."

Blue Eye make it happen, I hate responsibility,
Blue Eye hold me down, make it a possibility.
C'mon mate notice,
show me my reflection in your eyes.

Show me something, show me smile,
show me harbour, show me style,
show me stories, show me anima,
show me ships, show me stamina,
show me gladiator, show me wild,
show me old, show me child,
show me family, show me friend,
show me beginning, show me end,

show me adventure, show me rope,
show me lighthouse, show me hope,
show me voice, show me singing,
show me confetti, wedding bells ringing,
show me mansion, show me cat,
show me the key to our council flat,
show me legs, show me strength,
cast your rope, show me length,
show me stay, show me go,
show me a way to say hello.

Show me stupid, show me wise,
Blue Eye hold me down, notice.

Hey Blue Eye I've this notion of a lighthouse
on stubborn windswept rock and get this,
we're not afraid of tidal waves.
You've rope round your neck and saved a drowning man.
Blue Eye you look great in waders.
I'm wet and a bit Kate Bush.
You're sweating, dripping in inspiration.
Oh Blue Eye I could sing you to oblivion then eat you for breakfast.
You spear fish, I grill it, drink beer, your favourite,
and we bathe in the heat of the Aga.
Candlelight abstracts us and I'm where fairy tales are born.
You do funny voices, make shadow fingers, we're drunk on it all.
It's laughter like seagulls then everything stops.
Everything stops, it never stops stopping,
all we hear is the storm.

And you know what Blue Eye,
in candlelight you've that look, a twinkle,
and I'm wishing on a star in the bluest of skies
as if by magic you notice, take responsibility, hold me down.
I see my reflection in your eyes.

A Summer Night's Daydreaming

Learning to swim in nightmares,
they gossamer like whispers at a funeral,
like hanging on a thread.
Here the dead spin murky allusions on life.
"We might not be, but the night's still young."
Sound like gay men at the gym and spiders.

The night, lip-glossed by moonbeams and streetlights,
a great welcoming mouth,
the full-tongued shiny smile of a serial thriller,
licks its lips, vampire, ready to swallow and digest.

I'm impressed for it seems night is the day in drag,
an eye-shadowed world where shadows splutter
bad patter with a neon stutter,
blinking in 'n' out a lip-sync'd end of an era
and rat drowned dawn of a gutter.

Dancing's alive, a rave of shadows
where stories blur and real, freefall, shadow-land and feel,
imprinting dreams and subconscious with the murder
of nine to five.

It reverberates, regurgitates,
a time tunnel mystery, mad, bad, dangerous to know.
The sophisticated boom boom of its rock and roll,
the sultry smooth smooth smooth of its tainted soul
seldom heard,
it doesn't care.
There's no shortage of feet and handbags to accompany its rhythm.

It's not a velvet suited seducer, saturnine and charming,
it's a tutor,

a genderless S&M whore self-harming,
teaching to pay for pleasure and get pain for free,
where we trailblaze nothingness and fade in fade out
to the cautious threadbare hungover yawn of mourning.

The night has arms strong, alluring,
embracing the silks of infinity.
Obsesses, prepossesses, turning your head around,
twistin' your melon like a mirror-ball moon.

The sound of sirens arresting,
wail of dark romance and corruption;
love isn't everything, won't save the day or conquer all.
Right now the amorality of immortality
really does seem hair's breadth possible.

The night, intangible solid of Hellfire Clubs,
strip joints and sorcery.
Same scenes played out for centuries,
pornography putting the sound of mind ill at ease.
"Mummy where's the trees?"

And with no memory of sunbeams
Edith Piaf sings the breeze.

Monster Me

And then there's this monster me,
he's a lurker,
sits precariously edged on the polystyrene ledges
of Star Trek sets and breakdowns.
Hungers for what he thirsts for and eats china cups of teas.
Monster me is grumpy, Monster Me has fleas.

Skin's so stubborn he's forgotten how to scratch,
eyes so icy sees only cold.
He'd make a summer day pay tax,
the young old.

Monster Me keeps ideas gurgling in the back of his throat,
chokes on truth.
Sticks his dentures in Coca Cola
so he can continually mourn his youth.
Has a family of ghost kids, his parents in the shade.
Monster Me said he'd foster me but only if I paid.

Monster Me flashbacks to times he won't remember,
those nuclear times of Hell on Earth
and mushroom clouds in December.
Monster Me won't have a Christmas tree nor shed a birthday tear,
Monster Me's so bored of failing he's forgotten fear.

Monster Me eats pillows to muffle sounds of crying.
Monster Me ponders the delicate art of dying,
ponders how it's lifeless yet how it makes him dance,
go full throttle on the bottle given half a chance.
He'd swim through the air to hear that concrete crack.
Spirit's been broken, why shouldn't his back.
His dreams made rubble, hopes dashed,
liver failing,
flat trashed.

Monster Me follows me to the naughty step of my wishes.
Monster Me talks to me of eternity then pisses.

The Day An Innocent Ate My Mum

Ever felt so light you outshine the sun,
run so fast you leave the wind behind,
colourful as the firework display on an artist's pallet?
Ever felt so something you can outdo everything?
I did and I'll tell you when.
It was Thursday, Thursday week.
Some people say a week on Thursday,
doesn't bother me, their speak.
Honestly, people can say what they want to say
I'm not the speak police.
Anyway, it's Thursday week, the world's falling to pieces,
and that's when it happened, the impossible happened,
honest to God the impossible happened.
That was the day an Innocent ate my mum.

It was all so fast.
He was blonde, unseen,
kiss curls like cascading ivy, honey ivy not green,
the height of summer and yet butter wouldn't melt.
Nico sung his eyes while Aesop told his soul.
He was spun magical and singing gold,
trilling tunes of merry-go-rounds 'n' robins,
spinning spiders' webs from gossamer grey to candyfloss.

The Innocent's well boss, bosser than dogs.
It was Thursday, Thursday week.
I know cos that's when mum gets her family allowance.

She was angry, so angry,
thinks I don't know. I know.
She was late for her script, methadone's run low,
she was all a-fluster and blaming me.
There was even a smack.
Didn't hurt and even if it did it didn't.

Another reason I knew it was Thursday.
You see it only happens Thursday, every Thursday week.

She was calling my nan for everything and crying all the time,
I hate that.
Of course I was no good;
I'm never any good, always in the way.
Nan would have called her stupid and bought me a toy.
Love my nan, hate that day.
Every Thursday week nan's the better mum.
Mum says she's like me,
always nagging, getting her own say.

So, I was looking in Sparx window, looking a bit beyond it
and once again I saw him, he saw me
only this time he stepped from it.
I called him the Innocent cos I didn't know his name.
It was Thursday, it was Sparx shoe shop.
I knew it was Sparx cos it sold meffy shoes,
kinda shop people called Jeffrey use.
Thursday week you see, it's the only time we're there.
It was full of Spoonys, Wedges, Platforms and Kickers,
time hadn't stopped in Sparx or moving quicker
it was just slowly walking, almost stalking.

The Innocent was smiling and talked to me in kid.
"Do you want me to eat your mum?"
And honest to God, no word of a lie,
cross my heart and hope to die, that's what he did.

Hair turned into rats' tails, flailing, lashing,
skin started to scale green with purple freckles.
His bee-stung lips burning berry-red just like Dr Jekyll's,
skin like leather and a mouth that dripped blood.
It went smile, shark wide to Tyrannosaurus,
snarling, drooling, gnashing, no one but me saw us.

There was such a raw it could deafen Big Ben
or foghorns down the docks and no one could hear us.
His eyes became the size of saucers,
flying saucers, raging flying Tyrannosaucers
shooting real live laser beams, realer than dinosaurs and planes.

Mum was scraping skies, kicking bags, going off the rails,
kicking off about that stupid doctor again.
She calls the doctor crap, but he's a nice doctor who pats me noggin,
always gives me a lollipop.
She's really doing my head in. Hate her when she does that.
Love lollipops though. If she's angry I might not get my lollipop.
"Now?" the Innocent said.
I nodded back.
And with one snap of his powerful mouth
he bit off her head.

The peace was louder than Big Ben and the foghorns
and I lay on the pavement soaking up the sun.
The Innocent was chewing on my mum,
chewing her like gum.
He kissed my forehead. "You deserve a rest."

And you know,
just for a moment, I was outshining the sun,
leaving the wind behind,
painting my own firework display without the crash and bang.
At last I was outdoing everything.

The Innocent lay beside me, we giggled about farts.
He said I could her have back whenever I want.
I said
"Never on Thursdays, especially Thursday week,
because that's when all our fun stops
and end of the world starts."

A Trilogy Of Tramp

When young and still infectiously Catholic, me Ma would say to me, "Always be kind to tramps Gerard, as you never know lad, they just might be God in disguise." As advice goes, I think that's the most poetic. Well Ma, 'ere they are, your vagrant gods.

1. Bingo Jesus

A shabby man, my creation,
whose baggy shadow dances jigs long forgotten,
whose dreadlocks seem underlit by multicoloured neon.
He beams a smile unable to pinpoint memory,
his face a relief map, a bumpy wrinkled journey
of everyone's encounter with breath.
No stranger to death,
bored of the finite wisdom
of the successful dim and distant world weary.

It's whispered he can speak in tongues
this son of me, but doesn't have much to say,
he can walk on water,
but there's no way he'd be reduced to parlour tricks
for poets, story tellers hungry to be remembered.
He's offended by restrictions of longevity
and thinks immortality blinks for time wasters.

For Bingo Jesus, holy water is methylated spirit,
spirit making miracle lights gather.
A firefly disco ether
where he's always one step ahead of the flautists.
A favourite of tourists 'n' children whose giggles he knows
may one day mimic the shortcomings of his chest.
He's the best at this street theatre of polystyrene tea and sympathy,
of unintelligent bourgeois empathy
and broken tambourines.

2. Old Willow Pantomime

Walks like toppling,
a determined wobbling,
his unfurnished face mashed an elegant craggy chic.
An altered state, acquired taste,
more up and becoming than down and out.
Walks tall and forever,
killer smile and top hat sets him apart,
a gentleman.
Smells of damp, old clothes, booze and heart,
and rides a tricycle that can't be rode by anybody else.
A rickety rollicking, plinkety plonky ring ring of a thing
that just could save the world in a film,
if that film was about magic tramps and wobbly trikes.
He's like magic gone horribly wrong or maybe horribly right.
A spell conjured by a dark time child
who can't think what to do with midnight.

Old Willow Pantomime collects things,
sells battered tin, finds wedding rings.
In his bag a collapse of people's pasts and presents,
some broken, some near new, some pretending,
some still unwrapped would you believe.
Most need mending.
Gifts untouched by humane hands.
So much for gifts.

Time sifts.

It's amazing what you find when looking for nothing.
Be an entrepreneur if he smelt of roses,
but he smells of damp, old clothes, booze and body odour.

Old Willow Pantomime's read *Ulysses*, thinks he's cracked it.

Old Willow Pantomime dreams of sailing, boozing
and sharing the treasures of his seven seas.
The dawns and sunsets validating sight,
the invincible young men of the Africas, dancing on beaches,
fucking in dunes, waking in gutters, walking at night and drinking.
There's always been the drinking.
Aaaah, those were the days where apart from taking orders
and apart from the captain and apart from your duty
and apart from the war you were totally free.

Old Willow Pantomime misses the sea,
the war, its history,
its anarchy and promise of anything.

Old Willow Pantomime limps,
knows he's not long to tow the line.
Oh he'll be fine.
"How wrong's a piece of string?" he laughs.
"How wrong's a piece of thinking?"
He thinks instead of crying but there are jobs to be done
cos there's booze to be drunk,
there's always those pesky thoughts to be thunk
and things to be found and sold.

Old Willow Pantomime feels old, older than anyone else.
Some fingers ain't bending, joints aren't mending,
can't see past his nose but knows when something's shining.
Old Willow Magpie,
wrapped against the breeze in his crow cloak.

Brittle old soak,
looks to the Mersey and the moon,
feels its stillness, part of him rests with it.
Hears three teenagers singing show tunes,
he's smiling, read *Ulysses*, thinks he's cracked it.

"Nothing sells more than nothing," he says,
and of course selling nothing means you've nothing to lose.

Oh, but the booze, there's always the booze,
it's all about the booze.

3. The Ballad Of Willow And Bingo

In this place where flautists produce manna not music
and flaunt it, dishevelled, blurred, the ghosts dance on.
To drums that drum beyond drumming,
they're two bums-a-bumming, a couple of swells
double-barrelled bang-bang,
quick as lightning flash and buckshot.

They're demanding you see without knowing,
without showing you know showing.

Just sowing seeds of bluff and thunder,
summer breeze bubbling under
blowing away cobwebs from the war planet Mars.
In this place of paradise lost and found children dream stars.
It's where glitter retires after grafting on Christmas cards,
where you lift the curse,
find a sow's ear in every silk purse if you're lucky.

Welcome to the ballad of Willow and Bingo,
of Panto and Jesus,
of costumed imaginings beyond your wildest.
Here they use clouds as welcome mats,
buff off soft shoe silver dust and watch it fall as snow
covering sleepy hamlets in bonfire afterglow
of ever so 'umble wintertime humbug.

Welcome to a dreamscape of teen angst and immortals.
Through its misty portals watch Jameses Dean and Joyce
rub egos with Methuselah.

Not homoerotica!
What a fellah bruised old Methuselah, older before his time,
found in a bier keller, dressed as Petronella,
bliss dead and fancy dressed in a vat of wine.
A real slam bam thank you ma'am bamboozler,
creator of the new Bohemia,
made up and cut down in the drunk of his prime.
Someone wrote an unfathomable, unflattering rhyme.
Brendan Behan, top bitch!

Welcome turvy and
"Run Topsy run, run from Simon of Legree."
See Buddha sitting on the garden fence,
cross-legged, clothes-pegged whispering sweet nothings to Shiva.
Watch them politely nod and agree to agree
they both got it wrong.

This is the song flautists play,
Willow and Bingo dance to, bells ding-dang-a-dong to,
rights wrong to,
that so often Scooby don't but on occasion Scooby do,
of word jazz and jangle animated.

Welcome to the ballad of Willow and Bingo,
of Pantomime and Jesus, of the downtrodden breathless
and the uptown breathers, where the toe-tapping teased
forgive the toe-curling teasers eking out a happy ever afterlife
with silver tongues and spiritual tweezers.

Heaven.

The Imagination Is God

Light years shine heavy in maverick landscapes of lazy days
and jewelled summers.
They Doctor Who and Rock Folly,
meandering travellers lurk languidly in time,
philandering rhymes chock-a-block
and scissor-kiss a cock-eyed melancholy.
Ordinary people press their ears to the wall,
there's a sound, a whispering.
"The imagination is God. The imagination is tell-tale.
The imagination is all,"
said the girlfriend of the criminal clown
to the bog-eyed spruced-up dirty old town,
said the man going up to the man going down,
"The imagination is God."

The imagination is God.
Created God, and says "You can live forever."
Until you die.
Sing-song intonation of a Newcastle Wey-Aye,
a swansong petit pois in a rhubarb pie
set lovingly on a table levitating above soup.
Rhubarb soup!
Wey-Aye!
"The imagination is God, it's a hula hoop,"
giggled the old man at his old man's group.
Said the care worker he prodded to the vicar he bothered,
to the other old men who in unison nodded
"The imagination is God, it's a hula hoop."
The imagination is a care worker
working for an old man giggling at his old man's group.

The imagination is God.
In February you can fly it backwards over the January sales
and be first in the queue.

Buy a seed, plant it in love, watch it Bloom-Bang-A-Bang,
watch it Lulu.

It's the man who sold the world for a tenner and a woggle.
Mistake it for a baby's first gurgle,
grace it with the thought it deserves,
swerve round Speaker's Corner without a verb.
The imagination is not only a boy scout,
a mouth, a sixties singing sensation or a stolen car,
a wish invested in a shooting star, the imagination is God.
The only bar open on Planet Me,
every eel destined to party in the Sargasso Sea,
an Emma Peel fantasy.
The imagination can spell tarantula without the T.
 aran ula.
See!

The imagination is E. The imagination is we.
The imagination is God.

I'd like to tell you a story. It's about the spaces between words.

Once upon a time...

And they all lived happily ever after. I think.

A Meeting Of Minds

Scene: A quaint Victorian café in the middle of nowhere (that's the thing with written down nowheres, they're always an absurdly narrative somewhere). We know we're slap bang in the middle of whatever this particular nowhere is because of a cheap 1970s BBC special effect surrounding a badly superimposed building, a flashing on/off blue pulsing glare taken from an of-the-time revolving disco light. The building's a café called Kim by the Sea. Inside, several laced and lavendered old ladies are busying their dusty Edwardian-garbed magic around a selection of impossible sponges, intrepid fancies and occasional fruit pies. And, with buns of steel, there is one waiter: the physically magnificent Paolo. He is Spanish and devastatingly handsome, a stoically bold beauty that has never had to bother with the word ugly or its historically informed psychological repercussion/disintegrations. Sitting sipping Earl Grey tea at the only table in the café is a demure yet solid figure that, apart from a pair of orange training shoes, is clad head to toe in gingham. She seems somewhat haughtily aloof and a little disgruntled. The occasional slightly agitated flick of her black bob wig suggests she's waiting for someone but doesn't want anybody to know it. Even in an empty café in another celestial dimension, she appears to be performatively 'on'.

Paolo: Miss Poems, can I get you anything else?

Chloe: I don't know... can you?

Paolo: That's what I'm here for.

Chloe: Is it though, is it? Is that, is this, am I, what you're really here for?

Paolo: I'm pretty sure right now, yes. Why wouldn't it be? I'm a waiter and you need waiting on. It's been like this at Kim by the Sea for endless centuries.

Chloe: How long's a piece of thought?

Paolo: As long as you think it to be.

Chloe: If only it were that easy.

Paolo: I think it safe to assume it never is.

Chloe: Of course Paolo, no matter how definitely narrative or haphazardly accidental, we're all throwaway plot-points at the end of the day. Perhaps it's the ignoble duty of every great star to be kicked out of a speeding taxi like a drunken nun abusing Sister George. There I was thinking myself an irreplaceable poetic force of supernature and I'm just another hopelessly pissed lesbian bowsey as played by the late great Beryl Reid.

Paolo: Except you are not lesbian.

Chloe: Horses for courses Paolo, horses for courses.

Paolo: You seem to be thinking a great deal, Miss Poems. Thinking is good but it can take a toll, it's your insecurities controlling you. Could I perhaps offer you a relaxing neck cushion, an aspirin or one of our many medicinal liqueurs?

Chloe: I don't need any of anything, I'm fine. Whatever fine means when having to say goodbye to oneself. I'm as I always am, gelignite effervescent, endlessly knowing and more than a tad irritated. If I am to be hurled out of a cab just off a Fulham Broadway roundabout, then at least the hurler could have the good grace to be on time.

Paolo: I'm sure Mr Potter will be here soon. He is often a little confused but I've never known him not turn up.

Chloe: You know he's coming?

Paolo: Mr Potter tells me everything.

Chloe: Of course he does. If I may I be so bold Paolo, Mr Potter's a very lucky man.

Paolo: You should tell him that, sometimes he forgets.

Chloe: With you in tow he'd be a fool to.

Paolo: Oh it's nothing like that Miss Poems, we're just acquaintances. Thoughts, irreverent electrical transmissions passing through dreams.

Chloe: Why Paolo, with you, even a mere acquaintance would seem as a torrid romance, and please don't get me started on dreams. [*To herself*] Another of his universal rentboys, no doubt.

Paolo: You, as you always do, Miss Poems, flatter me.

Chloe: I'm sure there's a lot to flatter.

Paolo: I've had no complaints. This is my characterfully constructed designation, my role if you will, and it's safe to say Miss Poems, I fill it well.

Chloe: [*Blushing and twittering*] Oh Paolo, you make it like one doesn't know where to put oneself. Why, I'm all of a gingham fluster.

Paolo: Ahh, that's better Miss Poems, animated you are so attracting. Like an alluring flame might a needing moth.

Chloe: You do make me squirm so. Good squirming of course, not bad, never squelching.

Paolo: If you've a couple of minutes I could perhaps take you into the kitchen and show you our new condiment containers. They're in the comedic shapes of minibuses and ice cream vans.

Chloe: How municipally ornate. Yes, I'd love to see your minibuses.

Paolo: And ice cream vans.

Chloe: Sorry, and ice cream vans. I adore all forms of miniaturised motor vehicles. Vintage?

Paolo: Of course.

Chloe: There are few in this world as handsome and as decoratively astute as you, Paolo. Who knows, perhaps we may share a ninety-niner or two.

Paolo: Perhaps, shall we?

Chloe: Let's.

Suddenly there's a sound of a wildly peeling antiquated brass shop bell. From a spiralling void enters Gerry Potter. Although travelling through a windless/weatherless vortex, it's as if he's been fighting off a series of hellish non-negotiable twisters. He is in his late forties, handsome in a careless half-worn way. He has a grizzly yet camp appearance, like he doesn't take time and its repercussions seriously, or indeed changed his clothing for some while. There's a lot of eccentric bluster surrounding him, yet still an air of experiential, unthreatening authority. He's brushing himself down, dusting himself off and starting all over again.

Gerry: Blinkin' 'eck, oh fuckin' 'ell, well that was right off its 'ead, wasn't it! Crap, crap, and more crap. Ooh, oh and ow, for cryin' out loud. I'm really sorry about this. Please, don't mind me, it's just incredibly difficult hopping off one series of complex mindsets into another. Like taking a walk through several nervous breakdowns; doable, but you have to be prepared and I didn't bring a metaphorical brolly, so to speak. Never ordinarily knowing where I am makes not at all knowing where I am just that bit flakier. I'll be fine in a min. Wow, nice place, old and kind of stereotypically heavenly... I could murder a line or a Guinness, preferably both.

Chloe: Mr Potter, I presume.

Gerry: Ah, there you are, already here, how neat and tidy of you, please, call me Gerry.

Chloe: I'm Chloe. Chloe Poems.

Gerry: Oh I can assure you no one knows that more than me. *[There's a moment of connected recognition]* Oops, look at that, we're the same height.

Chloe: Of course we're the same height. You thought me a giant?

Gerry: Yes.

Chloe: I'm sorry to disappoint, shall we take tea?

Gerry: I'm not in any way disappointed and tea's fabulous.

Chloe: Do you have a blend in mind?

Gerry: Same as you babe.

Chloe: Paolo, we shall have to leave the exploration of your novelty shaped cruets for another time. Tea for two, Earl Grey if that's no bother.

Paolo: That would be fine.

Chloe: And a selection of your finest fancies, as I fancy our Mr Potter here has rather a sweet tooth.

Gerry: You fancy right, I'm anybody's for an old-fashioned 1970s knickerbocker glory. [*Paolo sets out to get the teas and fancies; on his way to the kitchen he catches Gerry's eye*]

Paolo: Mr Potter!

Gerry: Paolo! [*There's a small pause of something between them both and Paolo quickly leaves*]

Chloe: Do I detect a palpable frisson of involvement?

Gerry: Nothing so dramatic. Paolo is just someone I long to be.

Chloe: You want to be your own handsome hero?

Gerry: Not quite so devastatingly good looking and as masculine presenting, but something like that, yes. [*Gerry sits*]

Chloe: [*To herself*] When Paolo suggested his narcissism knew no bounds, I had no idea.

Gerry: Sorry, what was that?

Chloe: Nothing. Just a little Earl Grey stuck between my teeth. [*They both laugh politely*]

Gerry: Well, it's great to meet you, finally. I've always felt we've often nearly bumped into but never quite banged, if you know what I mean.

Chloe: What a vulgar analogy.

Gerry: I am from Liverpool. [*Pause*]

Chloe: I'm aware why you're here, how could I not be, so if you don't mind I shan't over-enthuse or jolly around small talking gibberish. Anyway, too acquired manners bore me.

Gerry: Yeah, me too.

Chloe: Under the circumstance you can forgive me my reticence toward you. As you can, indeed are, imagining, I'm a little ill at ease with what might unfold. Being a creature of thought, I'm not as au fait with the ultimate shape of outcomes as, say, others.

Gerry: I completely understand.

Chloe: You understand do you?

Gerry: I'm under no illusion about today.

Chloe: How instantly brutal!

Gerry: What?

Chloe: Soon as you're sat down, you are calling me illusion?

Gerry: Good God, no.

Chloe: "I'm under no illusion about today", I just heard you say it. If you were here to fix the plumbing, if you were indeed a plumber, I'd pass it by, but you're not a plumber, you're a fucking poet. Poets never use words like illusion unless they mean a contrasting minxy something else. They're a constant and addicted haunted by the transformative delusional hyper-lucidities of metaphor and trickery.

Gerry: Seriously, there's no metaphorical trickery afoot that was me just clumsily stating where I mentally am with all this.

Chloe: With all what, my illusionary existence? My will she won't she, my fairground find the lady! Roll up, roll up, roll up and watch The Gingham Aunt Sally magically disappear!

Gerry: Maybe.

Chloe: "Maybe" he says, like I don't know.

Gerry: I know you know.

Chloe: And have for some time, perhaps even before you, but I don't hold the upper hand, the winning card, so to speak. How could I, when I can't hold the deck. Reality and its illusions, for what they're worth, are your neck of our woods, aren't they Mr Potter.

Gerry: When it comes to the bombastic realities of reality in many ways you're realer than me.

Chloe: Realer than you?

Gerry: Yes.

Chloe: Realer than the great Gerry Potter?

Gerry: Less of the great babe, but yeah, I suppose so.

Chloe: Oh you suppose now do you?

Gerry: What I mean is, you're as real as you're sitting there. [*Chloe suddenly vanishes and reappears behind Gerry*]

Chloe: But I'm not, am I? [*Gerry turns to face Chloe*] Don't patronise me Mr Potter and please, while you've still a chance, have the decency to look me in the eye. I'm not, am I? [*Chloe vanishes and is back in her seat again*]

Gerry: I'd be able to look you in the eye a little easier if you'd keep still.

Chloe: Just proving a point, so let's honestly clarify shall we – am I realer than you?

Gerry: No. No, you're not. [*Pause*]

Chloe: Forgive me, this is hard.

Gerry: I know.

Chloe: I don't think you do. When you say goodbye, I shall simply disappear while you continue to exist.

Gerry: I'm aware of that.

Chloe: How can you be aware, how can you know what it's like to simply disappear?

Gerry: Well, you just magically disappeared and it was fine.

Chloe: Don't piss me off!

Gerry: Sorry, that was unnecessarily glib of me.

Chloe: Yes, it was.

Gerry: You know this is the final goodbye?

Chloe: Unless we're remaking James Whale's The Bride of Frankenstein, which I'm pretty sure we're not. Why else would the creator meet the created, the ego meet the alter?

Gerry: To soften the blow, to say goodbye properly with dignity. Ease the transition.

Chloe: You're saying it like this can be eased.

Gerry: We can try.

Chloe: This is not the end of one eccentric body morphing into another regenerational episode of your cheap sci-fi favourite Doctor Who. Nor is it the swapping over of an independent thinking, scintillatingly leather-clad Avenger girl. What are you going to do, pass me on the stairs with a sultry come-to-bed smile, whilst at the same time sensually advising me to stir my Earl Grey anti-clockwise? Then, with an expectant tap of your bowler, tell me it's all going to be ta-ra-ra-boom-di-ay? You may not have noticed, Mr Potter, but this is real life. [*Chloe vanishes and reappears the other side of Gerry*]

Gerry: I know and that's why I'm here. Believe it or not, it's hard for me too.

Chloe: How I loathe emotive sob stories, they do demean one. What next, the endless saga of ones continually depleting family?

Gerry: It's not a sob story, I don't do that shit.

Chloe: Don't you?

Gerry: No!

Chloe: Then what is it?

Gerry: The truth!

Chloe: Poets and truth, well ain't that an over-written too-decorative anomaly?

Gerry: I don't know what you mean.

Chloe: Nor do I, but it sounded suitably bitchy.

Gerry: I'm not here to bitch.

Chloe: I know, but maybe I am. You can't always have it your own way. Oops, sorry, silly me, you can. Ain't that just like a guy!

Gerry: I genuinely want this to a fair and reasoned conversation, none of this is about rejoicing anything, there isn't anything being achieved here. Especially anything as pathetically glib as simply getting your own way.

Chloe: Well done us, we're both glib.

Gerry: You've been such a mainstay for me over the past fifteen maybe twenty years. Through the drunken, drugged circusing haze of what some people some might ridiculously call a career, you were a no less than a gingham trailblazer.

Chloe: Spare me both the world-weary compliment and schmaltzy detritus, Mr Potter. I can assure you, suddenly caring for me isn't going to make not existing any easier.

Gerry: It's about more than care. It's knowing when to stop.

Chloe: When in doubt revert to an inarguable enigmatic. I'm a poet too, Mr Potter, I know the aim of pointed whimsy, inarguably enigmatic or otherwise.

Gerry: I'm not being inarguably enigmatic or pointedly whimsical, if anything I'm clumsily caring. I want this to be, well, something.

Chloe: Like what, a moment?

Gerry: Yes, if you like, a moment.

Chloe: So after all I've done and been, I'm reduced to the instantaneous ephemera of a too-romanced, overthought, constructed moment?

Gerry: Or elevated.

Chloe: You've a bold audacity, Mr Potter.

Gerry: So have you, Miss Poems.

Chloe: "Have", what an unfortunate word to use when all the time you meant "had". I "had" a bold audacity. Part tense, Mr Potter, on the back burner, fucked over, tossed aside, in a rickety old horse-drawn cart on uncomfortably bumping cobbles she's finally off to the knacker's yard.

Gerry: Yes, it's "had", past tense.

Chloe: Is it me or could you cut the tenses in this room with a knife?

Gerry: It's over. It's been over for some time. The world's changed, Chloe, it's bored of the truth. We rode the tail-end of a particular kind of political meltdown and for a while it was good. We did OK, then everyone got too scared, too Stepford, too Truman Show.

Chloe: Everybody or you?

Gerry: Both and neither.

Chloe: More ambiguous going nowhere conundrums, it's like living in Los Angeles.

Gerry: You became an increasingly lone, too honest voice in a world thinking it cleverer than the spin. We did it Chloe and did it brilliantly, but for us it's spun and we're done.

Chloe: So – take me out of the equation, remove me from societal discourse, abruptly silence any argument I may flagrantly have! How the fuck does that makes sense? The world still needs outsider voices.

Gerry: And it will still have one, just not yours. It's time to take away the flagrance; it now has to be my less flagrant Scouse timbre. It took a while for me to realise I can no longer do what I need to do with you, your voice, your image. Your voice has been leaving me for a while now Chlo', and these things have a time limit. We've anarchically said all we're creatively allowed.

Chloe: It's as Paolo's so often intimated, your arrogance is extraordinary.

Gerry: This is not about arrogance, it's the exact opposite.

Chloe: Pray tell Mr Potter, but how is telling somebody they've no longer the ability to exist anything but arrogant!

Gerry: You ruled me like a Boadicea of poetry, we were completely out there. Your poems, untouchable in both their rhythmic vivacity and crash bang walloping content. With you, all woads led to some extremely blue odes.

Chloe: Oh, so this is our special rose-tinted sepia moment is it, you're final big speech nothing more than pithily appalling puns? It's like being sat with a Christmas cracker.

Gerry: Let me finish, I've a lot to say and want to get it right and that's difficult with your constantly caustic interruptions.

Chloe: Oh, pardon me for breathing. Oh that's right, you're not going to!

Gerry: What?

Chloe: Pardon me!

Gerry: You were exalted and reviled in equal measure; I adored that about you. You were all the generously narcissistic arrogance I needed.

Chloe: Oh, so I'm the arrogant one now?

Gerry: That's not what I'm saying or mean. Of course it was always the arrogance of me creating the arrogance of you, now it's time to be my own new naked arrogance.

Chloe: Hark at the narcissist calling the kettle a narcissist... and you will be naked without me.

Gerry: And I'm hoping to embrace that.

Chloe: How thrillingly valiant.

Gerry: How predictably snide.

Chloe: Forgive me, as I appear to have lost some of my trademark ballsy physicality. It's terribly difficult to point the finger when you been disallowed a hand.

Gerry: Let me say what I've come to say, then you can lyrically bitch to your heartless content.

Chloe: If I must and I will.

Gerry: What was initially freeing between us, that strong, uniquely powerful, soaring theatricality, it was an uplifting wild, almost peformatively feral, until...

Chloe: Until?

Gerry: Until it eventually stopped being that and became kind of caged, tied up in its own self-fulfilling containment. Freedom, whatever that means, on its own becomes repetitive, without the necessary humanity it starts to ring a too-comedic hollow.

Chloe: How generous of you to liken me to an inhuman bell without a clapper.

Gerry: I could spend the rest of my life being yet another gingham petticoat under yet another gingham bodice, but sometimes y'know, you just gorra wear your own clothes and be your own animal.

Chloe: Oh for God's sake, someone dial whine whine whine and get the cliché police. Save it!

Gerry: Chloe, let's not do this.

Chloe: Why not? Think of it as our moment.

Gerry: I could think of better moments.

Chloe: Well at this moment, I think you're jealous.

Gerry: What?

Chloe: Jealous of my long standing, you can't cope I'm far more known than you. That I, Chloe Poems, Gay Socialist Transvestite Poet, The Gingham Diva, Voice of Treason, The Radical Agenda Bender, is somehow a bigger poetic entity than you are or ever will be.

Gerry: Don't be ridiculous.

Chloe: Truth's brutal intensities are always ridiculous to poets, it's why we selfishly re-augment truth, bend it to our will. A lie forged from truth is still somehow a truth isn't it, Mr Potter?

Gerry: That's as maybe, but I can assure you of one thing, I'm not jealous of some hammy drag queen!

Chloe: A ham drag!

Gerry: Exactly, I couldn't have put it better myself.

Chloe: Mistaking carefully sculpted heightened poetics for overacting is a rookie mistake!

Gerry: Not from where I'm standing; like watching Gielgud on steroids.

Chloe: Oh, I get it, you want to tone it down for an increasingly younger, less theatrically informed, more urban demographic!

Gerry: I've absolutely no interest in any kind of demographic, urban or otherwise.

Chloe: Perhaps, as you're growing older, entering middle-age and becoming more masc in appearance and voice, I, the younger, zhuzhier, vital you, am becoming more of an embarrassment, is that it? Are you wanting to take to the stage and wittily mansplain away my once powerful effeminacy?

Gerry: No! If I talk of you, I will speak with enormous fondness and respect.

Chloe: Give me a fucking break! Tell the bare naked truth, you're disgusted by and don't want to be an old drag queen.

Gerry: I don't want to be an old drag you!

Chloe: You're behaving like a typically boorish man, do you know that? Yes, man, I said man! Finally, poor little picked on puffy Gerry's a real balls-scratching, crotch-grabbing, grown-up man. Oh how wonderful, now he can do to vulnerable others what was done to vulnerable him; he too can try and rid the world of obvious effeminates.

Gerry: I've never thought of myself like that and never will.

Chloe: Oh shut up will you! This isn't an act of intellectual independence; it's yet another thinly veiled instance of self-loathing. You're queer bashing yourself, us both. More than that, you're enjoying it. What's it like being your very own homophobe? You useless, going nowhere, insanely brutal, fucking HOMOPHOBE!

Gerry: If being my own homophobe allows me to make difficult life-changing decisions, then it's actually quite pleasant, because living with the storm-clouding pomposity of your thundering opine has not only taken its toll, it's left me bored. [*Chloe's jaw drops*]

Chloe: How dare you!

Gerry: Yes, you heard me, bored, bored of your finger-pointing absolutism. Your increasingly immobile intellect, your sightless vision and overweening utopianism.

Chloe: Overweening utopianism... now that does take the biscuit! There's isn't anything remotely wrong in exquisitely presenting the raw boldness of hope.

Gerry: There are things I've got to say and they're not *your* things.

Chloe: But you are me!

Gerry: Yes, I'm you and yes, you're me, and I did/do believe in everything you've said/done, but ultimately we're not the same thing. Not anymore.

Chloe: You can say that again!

Gerry: Think of me as a souped-up, jazzy little jet-ski zooming away from an all out-at-sea, clapped-out, creaky old junk. Think of this as the divorce of the Howl and the Pussycat.

Chloe: If I were truly free and not at the drearily redundant whims of your tepid imagination then I should take this empty pot of Earl Grey and smash it over your craggy, baldy, Sid Jamesesque head.

Gerry: And if I had less restraint over my raging and increasingly colourful imagination then you would be hanging, swinging from that mock Tudor beam by a noose woven from your own gingham gown.

Chloe: So you're killing me off?

Gerry: You killed yourself!

Chloe: I am many things, but I am not a coward.

Gerry: Nor am I!

Chloe: Oh yes you are. I'm your easy way out aren't I, Mr Potter? A casually imagined yet carefully constructed meta-reality, what you can't do in real life, you can do inside your head. I'll be little more than faux Ortonesque blood-splattered deathscape, a lyrically witty story to endlessly bore potential lovers over candlelit seductioning dinners for two.

Gerry: I've never had a seducing candlelit dinner for two.

Chloe: Oh, I used to be Chloe Poems, y'know, The Gingham Diva, but I bit the drag bullet and bravely killed her off. Bludgeoned the silly bitch to death, stuffed her in a battered old holdall and now she resides under my bed. If you hear any strange screams throughout the night don't worry, it won't be me begging for more, just Chloe demanding to be let out for a piss.

Gerry: Well, I hadn't thought of that, but now you've said, I'll probably use it. It is quite funny. Y'never know babe, it might just bag me a bit of trade.

Chloe: Don't you ever call me "babe"!

Paolo enters with a trolley full of tea and cakes. The laced and lavendered old ladies are behind him, knuckledusters on clenched fists, sensing a fight.

Paolo: Fresh tea, Miss Poems. Earl Grey as ordered and, of course, your cakes.

Chloe: Thank you, Paolo.

Gerry: Yes, yes thank you.

Chloe: Sorry if things got a little vocally volatile, Paolo. It's just I'm about to enter oblivion and as you can imagine I'm fucking terrified.

Paolo: Oh, I understand the endless stretch of oblivion, Miss Poems. I'm no stranger to the void. I've longed to fly free and escape it for many a tortuous millennia.

Gerry: I'm sorry too, Paolo. You know me 'n' my big gob, Scottie Road 'n' all that.

Chloe and Gerry: I think it's safe to say we're both sorry.

Paolo: There really is no need to apologise.

Chloe: Paolo, where are the fancies? I ordered a selection of fancies.

Paolo: I'm sorry Miss Poems, we're fresh out of fancies. While you were arguing, the waitresses they got peckish and have eaten them all. When ravenous there's no controlling them, like unwieldy animals. All we have left is a selection of pies and I'm afraid a small one at that, just apple and humble. I thought some pie is better than no pie at all. Well, at least now you have choices.

Chloe: Oh!

Gerry: Fuckin' 'ell!

Chloe: Quite.

Gerry: Shit!

Chloe: Pie?

Gerry: I suppose.

Chloe: But what pies, eh Gerry.

Gerry: Indeed.

Chloe: Perhaps you should choose, Mr Potter.

Gerry: Ladies first?

Chloe: Well, in that case I rather fancy apple.

Gerry: Apple? I'm a little surprised.

Chloe: That's my choice.

Gerry: OK, I don't mind humble.

Chloe: What?

Gerry: Humble.

Chloe: Are you sure?

Gerry: Yes.

Chloe: I just thought...

Gerry: Why not. Think I've had it before. If not, I've never been frightened of new flavours.

Chloe: Nor I. I'm sorry but I have to say this, it's you don't strike me as somebody who naturally employs humility.

Gerry: I'm not, never have been, in so many ways I loathe it.

Chloe: That's exactly what I mean.

Gerry: I certainly find the newer concepts of what I consider to be societally-engined humility, psychologically controlling, hierarchically condescending and clearly asinine.

Chloe: That's where I was going with that.

Gerry: Can't help but think employers are using it to keep their workers grateful for what little they're giving them. Crumbs aren't just crumbs anymore. Now they're glorious crumbs, wonderful crumbs, thank you for the opportunity crumbs, but the thing is Chloe, I still see crumbs.

Chloe: Crumbs!

Gerry: To be completely honest with you, I find the current re-workings of humility and its gratuitous yelps of gratefulness not only sonically disappointing but culturally barbaric.

Chloe: Couldn't agree more, so why the humble pie now?

Gerry: Because this isn't overtly societally informed or actualised, is it. It's imaginatively between you and I. Forget what I said earlier because I have. I was nervously annoyed at us, at me, and of course you.

Chloe: Thank you, I aim to agitate.

Gerry: Of course you do.

Chloe: Did.

Gerry: Although this is goodbye, the bottom line is and has always been, I love you Chloe Poems. You've given me some of the most thrilling rides of my life. There's a certain something about being somebody else, someone like you, I don't think most people get to know. I'm not saying everybody should find the magical jig of drag here, but I am confidently saying, I'm glad I did.

Chloe: Me too.

Gerry: I've always loved and held dear childhood notions of things like lycanthropy, the animalistic changing from one form to another. Superheroes, changing from everyday drab dress to brightly coloured, eye-catching, fly-highing costumes. Werewolves and superheroes are much the same things to me and I always wanted to be one.

Chloe: I think that rather lovely.

Gerry: When young and life was hard, I was haunted by both the joyous and dangerous possibilities of change. I instinctively knew there was an untalked of and fabulous mischief to be had with it. I never thought it would ever be easy and it wasn't. In fact, looking back, easy was the boring part.

Chloe: Absolutely it is.

Gerry: With you, I finally got to do the not boring part, I mischievously changed. Not into a werewolf or a superhero, but something not unlike, something similar.

Chloe: So, you're saying I'm a cross between an Amazonian

Wonder Woman and a flesh-devouring mythic beast?

Gerry: Oh, most definitely if not defiantly, yes. I think as children most gay men, certainly gay men my age, were tortured by metamorphosis, because the shapes we were given as kids, they didn't fit, none of it ever fitted me. So, to one day be able to choose, more than that even, the bonkers journeying of it all. The realisation and finding out you can choose, that all that out there mind-bending, body-shaping possibility could be yours. Well, it was wondrous.

Chloe: You know something, I don't think I've ever had to choose anything. Whatever it is has always been there, right in front of me.

Gerry: That's because you were the choice.

Chloe: I feel somewhat flattered.

Gerry: You were – *are* – wondrous. People loved, people hated, people stood in rapturous ovation and people angrily stomped out of the auditorium. But for me and more than anything else, you gloriously epitomised the dizzying power and improvisational clarity of decision. You weren't a new pair of shoes, a new car or a dancing all night drug-infused holiday destination, you were another human being. Not just that, a superhuman being, one who would cause and revel in so much chaotic reaction. We're talking proper eye of the storm stuff here; you were completely free. How many people are ever that volcanically expressive?

Chloe: I've no idea.

Gerry: No you, and I think innocently, don't. There's a naturally built-in anarchic thrust to drag, an explosive world changing, world creating/shaping energy/synergy that's hardly discussed. Maybe it can't be and there lies its damning hell-firing on all cylinders secret. It's totally off its head, an out the ballpark wild, rude, sexy, raging, musical, wonderfully rhythmic, louche, searing, primal screech. Is there anything in this world louder, more sparkling than a confident not-giving-a-fuck on the mic drag queen? It doesn't, nor should it, give a flying fuck about anyone or anything, and to embody all that, actually *be* it, well, who does?

Chloe: My oh my, Mr Potter. Well, I wasn't expecting that.

Gerry: Is that a single tear I see before me?

Chloe: Yes, it is, but it's a jealous tear because you got that monologue and I didn't. Not terribly humble of you.

Gerry: Yes, you're right, so here's the humility. I learnt that monologue from you. You taught me how to grab the mic, the spotlight and dominate in it. I could never have done that by myself.

Chloe: You make me sound omnipotent.

Gerry: I think the gender blending distortion of drag is.

Paolo: May I suggest, as there are more than enough servings of both pie, you to try a little of each?

Chloe: You know, after all this emotional kafuffle I seem to have lost my appetite. And you, Mr Potter?

Gerry: Actually Chloe, I'm suddenly a little more peckish than before. I would like some pie.

Paolo: Well, there's more than enough apple pie, Mr Potter.

Gerry: No, Paolo. I'll stick to humble.

Paolo: Cream?

Gerry: I'll take it as it comes. [*Paolo starts to slice the humble pie*]

Paolo: Is that enough?

Gerry: Perhaps a little more.

Paolo: My, that's quite a slice.

Gerry: It's quite a moment.

Paolo: What is?

Gerry: Our conversation, our jangle.

Paolo: But you're talking to yourself.

Gerry: Am I? Well?

Paolo: No, no you're not. You're full of impossible jingle jangle, Mr Potter.

Gerry: Paolo, there's an auld Liverpool saying: there's no point jangling if you don't hear the jingle.

Paolo: There is?

Gerry: No, like everything else here, I just made it up.

Chloe: May I interrupt you two love birds?

Paolo: Of course.

Chloe: Me too.

Paolo: Sorry?

Chloe: I wish to change my order, I'm allowed that aren't I? After all, it is my last meal.

Paolo: You may do whatever you wish.

Chloe: [*To Gerry*] One question.

Gerry: Only the one?

Chloe: Will I disappear forever?

Gerry: Corporeally, yes. I will never be you again, but that doesn't mean I won't write you.

Chloe: You mean like Dan Dare, Sherlock Holmes and Minnie the Minx?

Gerry: Yes, exactly like.

Chloe: That could be quite fun.

Gerry: I think so. I've got this great story that's perfect for narration in your voice.

Chloe: Was that all I ever was?

Gerry: What?

Chloe: A story, a voice.

Gerry: Good God, no. There are people out there who will never know who I am. People who were touched by your emboldening bravado and difficult truth. You have a very real and exciting history.

Chloe: I have?

Gerry: Yes. Have you ever been alone?

Chloe: An odd question right now, don't you think?

Gerry: No, I think it's the right question. Have you ever been alone?

Chloe: No. Wherever I'm around there's always someone about. Once there were only two people, in a grubby little hole, Edinburgh I think. Another time, at a park in London, there were maybe eighty thousand. Yes, there's always been someone. Well, there *was* always someone.

Gerry: And most of those people will have a story of you. You do exist.

Chloe: But I don't.

Gerry: You do and you don't.

Chloe: Like a myth?

Gerry: Yes, like a myth.

Chloe: The myth of you?

Gerry: No, the myth of *you*. You're the stuff of legend, Chloe Poems.

Chloe: Nonsense.

Gerry: Actually, that's more accurate. You're the stuff and nonsense of legend, Chloe Poems.

Chloe: Oh, Mr Potter, you're making me blush.

Gerry: And that has to be the first time that's happened. [*A moment*]

Chloe: The same as Mr Potter, Paolo. Humble, no cream.

Paolo: Are you sure, Miss Poems?

Chloe: Looks like I have to be.

Gerry: Thank you.

Chloe: No, Gerry Potter, [*taking a bite of pie*] thank you.

Gerry: My pleasure.

Chloe: Oh before I go. I'd like to ask, have you ever been alone?

Gerry: Yes.

Chloe: Will you be lonelier without me?

Gerry: Yes.

Chloe: Then why on eart— [*Chloe suddenly vanishes*]

Gerry: Wonder if I can do that; is my imagination after all. [*Gerry takes another bite of humble pie and with a camp arms-in-the-air operatic gesture promptly disappears, leaving just an echo of his voice*] Hope to see you soon, Paolo.

Paolo is sat on the floor trying to levitate a table. The table judders slightly and lifts a millimetre. Paolo thrilled by his success broadly smiles. He looks around; there's nothing there, just the ghosts of echoes. He just about catches the last repeating "Paolo" of Gerry's fond farewell.

Paolo: And I hope to see you too, Mr Potter.

We hear a sharp crack of bone and dull snap of skin. There's a hackle of giggling, gradually lessening, from the now slowly disappearing laced and lavendered old ladies. Under Paolo's jacket he is beginning to sprout wings.

The End

Outroduction: This Is My Marrie Barrie Universe

I first met Maria Barrett in 1979. My, that was damn fine year. She was very young and attending The Everyman Youth Theatre's junior group. At the height of anarcho post-punk nu-wave, she was proudly sporting a white/blue Edwardian sailor dress. Brian and I fell instantly in love with her and she would become our dear friend. It was a no-brainier to get her to write an introduction for this book, so in keeping I dedicate this Outroduction to her. When we're together, something caustically magical happens; it's kinda indefinable but oft' noticed. It's ancient and new, kindred and always hysterical. You should see her, pissed off with my drunken arrogance end-of-the-night power-flounce. Nobody does it better.

Ancient like beginnings, stars of things ending,
engines of things starting, big 'n' bangin'!

We're culturally tattooed in stellar-clubs and Chinese restaurants,
super nova'd 'n' soup noodle'd.
We have roar and splendour of theatre,
ovation of kinship
and are nightly lamplit shined by our city.

Catholicism sensually un-beads its zipped-up rosary
'n' we were crucified by that dead-fit scally's bona lals.
You swore he dropped his trackies just for us.

Remember that day the planet changed and we knew it,
stepping off a bus into another dimension?
It was almost like we'd never been to confession.
Cackle-tripping through that blizzarding Narnia.
What a wonderfully hallucinogenically informed palaver!

Marrie Barrie,
we were Tomorrow People then,
we're then people now.
We've always had that sense of something,
of somewhere, other and else, of universe.

I'm remembering our arguing,
how all gays are ours… especially yours.
How the packed pub's housing just us two,
it's our stage, our double act, double-gin'd and Guinness'd.
White-hot 'n' molten, coral-pink lippy 'n' floating,
we're Jimmy Cagney boasting
"Top o' the bill 'n' the world Ma,"
toasting events arising.

Feel sorry for people watching, but they are getting a free show.
We do all the voices,
pull all the faces and the barman.
We're being terribly good at being theatrically brusque
and we know.

All aglow when remembering what we've been through,
people gone, the fondly recalled not-forgotten.
Way we eye-contact resurrecting Brenda.
It's an out 'n' proud partying séance when we're rotten.

We whip sad because we flog happy and in there's the rub.
On damn spot-light!
Remembering so many things,
the dancing, Jody's,
eye of the storm of 'Chain Reaction',
spiral pour of cascading language, its wit 'n' aim,
the wan tons, the chilli oil, the flounge.
The reaching for the stars, the hitting the ground.

What I'm recalling most
is my arm round your shoulders,
stocious in a bar and us howling.
You Elizabeth Taylor-made and me all Roddy McDowall'd-up,
telling you how much I adore you.